W9-BKA-260

Leaders of the Colonial Era

Benjamin Franklin

Leaders of the Colonial Era

Lord Baltimore

Benjamin Banneker

William Bradford

Benjamin Franklin

Anne Hutchinson

Cotton Mather

William Penn

John Smith

Miles Standish

Peter Stuyvesant

Leaders of the Colonial Era

Benjamin Franklin

William W. Lace

CHELSEA HOUSE
PUBLISHERS

An imprint of Infobase Publishing

Benjamin Franklin

Copyright © 2010 by Infobase Publishing

Chelsea House
An imprint of Infobase Publishing
132 West 31st Street
New York, NY 10001

Library of Congress Cataloging-in-Publication Data

Lace, William W.
  Benjamin Franklin / William W. Lace.
      p. cm. — (Leaders of the colonial era)
  Includes bibliographical references and index.
  ISBN 978-1-60413-737-8 (hardcover)
  1. Franklin, Benjamin, 1706-1790—Juvenile literature. 2. Statesmen—United States—
Biography—Juvenile literature. 3. Inventors—United States—Biography—Juvenile literature.
4. Scientists—United States—Biography—Juvenile literature. 5. Printers—United States—
Biography—Juvenile literature. I. Title. II. Series.

  E302.6.F8L33 2010
  973.3092—dc22
  [B]

                                   2010010205

Text design and composition by Kerry Casey
Cover design by Keith Trego
Cover printed by Bang Printing, Brainerd, Minn.
Book printed and bound by Bang Printing, Brainerd, Minn.
Date printed: September 2010
Printed in the United States of America

10 9 8 7 6 5 4 3 2 1

This book is printed on acid-free paper.

Contents

1

Young Ben Franklin

At the Constitutional Convention of 1787, one of the delegates was dared to clap General George Washington familiarly on the shoulder and give him a hearty greeting. The delegate did so, thus winning a good dinner, but declared after the withering look he received from the general in return that he would not do so again for a thousand dinners.

Indeed, many of the nation's so-called Founding Fathers appear similarly unapproachable in modern eyes. The austere, aloof Washington, intellectual Thomas Jefferson, caustic John Adams, and proud Alexander Hamilton are all difficult to accept as human beings with human emotions. They stare from portraits, statues, and the pages of textbooks—cold, grim, unsmiling.

Benjamin Franklin is the great exception. Here is a man one could picture joining for a meal, exchanging gossip, telling jokes, and arguing the finer points of science, religion, government, or a pretty girl at the next table. He had as brilliant a mind as any of his colleagues. But alongside evidence of that brilliance is a legacy of charm and wit with a dash of impishness and a reputation as a womanizer.

Franklin contributed mightily to the formation of the United States, making edits to the Declaration of Independence, skillfully negotiating an alliance with France during the American Revolution, and using his knowledge of human nature to achieve consensus on the nation's Constitution. His role was so important that he has been called the only president of the United States who was never president of the United States. But his fame rests equally on his achievements as a scientist, inventor, author, and publisher—quite a list for a boy from Boston who had only two years of formal education.

FAMILY BACKGROUND

Benjamin Franklin was born on January 17, 1706, in Boston, Massachusetts, to Josiah and Abiah Franklin. Josiah had sired seven children with his first wife, Anne, who came with him from England and died in 1689. Then there came ten more children with his second wife, Abiah, of which Benjamin was the eighth and the youngest son.

The Franklins had long been known as independent thinkers. Benjamin's Protestant great-great-grandfather, Thomas, kept a banned English Bible hidden on the underside of a stool during the persecution of Protestants by Roman Catholic Queen Mary I. Thomas's father had supported the rights of small farmers whose land was being taken over by aristocrats.

The early Franklins had other qualities that Benjamin would inherit, including a vast array of talents and an insatiable curiosity.

Franklin's grandfather, also named Thomas, was a skilled woodworker, gunsmith, surgeon, and notary. He was also an amateur historian and astronomer.

Franklin's father, Josiah, moved from the family farm at Ecton to the town of Banbury, where he became an apprentice to his older brother John, a dyer of cloth. Religion had divided the family. Some of the Franklins chose to remain with the official state church, the Church of England, but others, including Josiah, joined a new group that believed in what they considered a more pure form of Protestantism. The members of this group were called Puritans. In 1689, during a time when Puritans in England were restricted in their worship, Josiah and his family moved to Boston, expecting, as Benjamin Franklin wrote in *The Autobiography of Benjamin Franklin*, "to enjoy their mode of religion with freedom."

Boston was an ideal place for Puritans. The government of the Massachusetts Bay Colony was dominated by ministers, notably Increase Mather and his son Cotton, but there was not much demand in this somber city for the highly colored cloth that Josiah made. So he had to find a new occupation and settled on that of chandler, making candles and soap from animal fat.

The young Benjamin was, according to his *Autobiography*, "generally a leader among the boys" with whom he played on the banks of the Charles River. He was a strong and avid swimmer and twice used the river to demonstrate his ingenuity. Reasoning that if his hands and feet were larger they could push more water and give him more speed, he fashioned flippers made of wood. On another occasion he floated on his back while flying a kite to show that the kite could act as a sail, propelling him across the water.

Franklin was an early and voracious reader, writing in his *Autobiography* that, "I do not remember when I could not read." His keen mind was apparent to his father, who decided that his son should become a clergyman. Accordingly, he was enrolled at the

YOUNG BEN'S WHISTLE

Benjamin Franklin learned a hard lesson about thriftiness at the age of seven when he paid too much for a toy whistle. He recalled the incident in a 1779 letter to Madame Brillon, a French woman with whom he had a close relationship:

When I was a child of seven years old, my friends, on a holiday, filled my pocket with coppers. I went directly to a shop where they sold toys for children; and being charmed with the sound of a whistle . . . I voluntarily offered and gave all my money for one. . . . My brothers, and sisters, and cousins, understanding the bargain I had made, told me I had given four times as much for it as it was worth; put me in mind what good things I might have bought with the rest of the money; and laughed at me so much for my folly, that I cried with vexation; and the reflection gave me more chagrin than the whistle gave me pleasure.

This, however, was afterwards of use to me, the impression continuing on my mind; so that often, when I was tempted to buy some unnecessary thing, I said to myself, "Don't give too much for the whistle"; and I saved my money.

He went on to say that over the years he had seen many people "give too much for the whistle," including those who gave up every material comfort for the sake of wealth, those who yielded to bodily pleasures and ruined their health, and those who were so caught up with appearances that they spent themselves into poverty. "In short," he wrote, "I conceive that a great part of the miseries of mankind are brought upon them by the false estimates they have made of the value of things, and by their giving too much for their whistles."

age of eight in what later would become the Boston Latin School, where he quickly moved to the head of his class and then into the next class.

FINDING A TRADE

After Benjamin had been in school for a year, his father decided that a minister's education, which would have included nearby Harvard College, would be too expensive. Benjamin was sent to another, less prestigious school where he spent the next year excelling at writing but failing mathematics. That failure convinced Josiah that it was time for his son to learn a trade, and Benjamin's formal schooling ended.

So, at the age of 10, Benjamin went to work for his father. He disliked the chandler's trade and even threatened to run away and go to sea, so his father agreed to find something more appealing. Given Benjamin's love of books, Josiah proposed an apprenticeship with his older son James who, at 21, had just returned from England after being trained as a printer. The 12-year-old Benjamin, somewhat reluctantly, signed a contract that would bind him for nine years.

Benjamin quickly learned the mechanical aspects of printing. He was taught how to compose a printing plate letter by letter out of metal type, how to spread ink on the plate, and how much pressure to apply to transfer the ink properly to paper. It was a dirty job, and apprentices were usually so ink-stained that they were known as printer's devils.

Printers were also writers, and they published their own ballads, poems, pamphlets, and newspapers. James quickly put Benjamin to work as an author. He produced two poems, which he called "wretched stuff" in his *Autobiography,* and sold enough copies to "flatter my vanity."

Boston in 1718 was easily the most literate city in North America. It had a dozen booksellers while the other British colonies combined had none. Benjamin had access to books and made the most of it, continuing his education by borrowing books from booksellers' apprentices. He would sit up most nights reading so he could return the books in the early morning before anyone missed them.

From John Bunyan's *The Pilgrim's Progress* he learned that people can improve themselves through knowledge and by overcoming barriers. From *Lives* by the ancient Greek writer Plutarch he saw how individuals could shape great events, sometimes for good. Such ideas ran against the Puritan concept that humans were essentially corrupt and that each individual's destiny was predetermined by God.

Another book that influenced young Benjamin was *Bonifacius, or Essays to Do Good* by Cotton Mather, in which the clergyman called on citizens to create groups or associations to benefit the general population. The central core of Benjamin Franklin's moral code would later be the belief that people could improve themselves by working to improve the situations of others.

He often debated such matters with his close friend John Collins. At a young age Benjamin started to develop a style of argument that he would use when trying to win people over to his point of view. Instead of being confrontational, he would use a softer, more indirect approach, often exposing through gentle questions the weaknesses of his opponents' positions.

In 1721 James Franklin lost a contract to print a newspaper. He decided to publish one of his own, which he called the *New-England Courant*. The paper was independent, opinionated, and often disrespectful of established authority. James and other contributors sometimes followed the common practice of writing highly critical essays under assumed names to hide their true identity. Sometimes these articles were contributed anonymously so that even James did not know who had written them.

As a boy, Benjamin Franklin showed hints of genius. But when he began to fail mathematics, his father decided to end his formal education. Joining his father in the trade of candle making, young Benjamin was miserable.

SILENCE DOGOOD

Writing these critical essays was the perfect opportunity for Benjamin to practice his writing skills without his brother's knowledge. To offer his opinions, Benjamin invented Silence Dogood, a middle-aged widow of a country minister. In the first essay, Silence promised the *Courant*'s readers that she would provide "a short Epistle, which I presume will add somewhat to their Entertainment" every two weeks.

Disguising his handwriting, Benjamin slipped 14 essays under the *Courant*'s door between April and November 1722. Silence Dogood wrote about everything from family relationships to higher education to religion. She commented that Harvard students emerged "after Abundance of Trouble and Charge [cost], as great Blockheads as ever, only more proud and self-conceited." Another time, she wondered whether more damage was done "by hypocritical Pretenders to Religion, or by the openly Profane?"

The sprightly language, pointed opinions, and crackling wit of Widow Dogood were all the more remarkable because they came from the pen of a 16-year-old boy. Moreover, they were, writes Walter Isaacson in *Benjamin Franklin: An American Life*, one of the first examples of typical American humor, "the wry, homespun mix of folksy tales . . . perfected by such Franklin descendants as Mark Twain and Will Rogers."

When Silence Dogood finally revealed her true identity, the other *Courant* contributors were amazed and delighted—except for James. In his *Autobiography*, Franklin wrote that the revelation "did not quite please" his brother, who "thought, probably with reason, that it tended to make me too vain."

Early in 1723 Benjamin got another chance to write. James wrote an essay so critical of the religious establishment that the Massachusetts General Court issued an order prohibiting him from publishing the *Courant*. To get around the order, James decided to publish the newspaper under Benjamin's name. Since naming James's apprentice as publisher would not be acceptable to the court, the existing apprenticeship contract was publicly canceled and a new one was secretly signed.

From January to May 1723, with James in hiding, Benjamin published the *Courant*. He wrote under his own name and others, such as Timothy Wagstaff and Abigail Twitterfield. One memorable article, quoted in H.W. Brands's *The First American*, showed Benjamin's aversion to pompous authority. It pointed out that even in the Bible "we never read of Noah *Esquire* . . . nor the *Right Honourable* Abraham."

James was acquitted in May and returned to the *Courant*. He resumed treating Benjamin like an apprentice, including an occasional beating. The younger brother later admitted in his *Autobiography* that he probably earned the beatings by being "too saucy and provoking." In September 1723, fed up with his brother and having sold some of his books to earn his passage, Benjamin secretly boarded a ship bound for New York.

PHILADELPHIA

New York's only printer, William Bradford, did not have a job for Benjamin, but urged him to proceed to Philadelphia to seek employment with Bradford's son, Andrew. Benjamin arrived in Philadelphia on October 6. According to his *Autobiography*, he was "fatigued with travelling, rowing, and want of rest . . . very hungry; and my whole stock of cash consisted of a Dutch dollar and about a shilling in copper."

Benjamin addressed his hunger by buying three pennies worth of rolls from a baker and eating them as he walked through the city. On Market Street, he passed the home of John Read. There he saw Read's daughter Deborah watching him from the front door.

Benjamin would later marry Deborah. The young woman, "saw me and thought I made, as I certainly did, a most awkward, ridiculous appearance," he later wrote.

As it turned out, Andrew Bradford did not need another employee, but he said that Samuel Keimer, a printer new to Philadelphia, might. Benjamin did not think much of Keimer's abilities. He felt that Keimer was good enough at setting type but knew next to nothing about presswork. Benjamin promptly put Keimer's press in working order and began work as a journeyman, one who is beyond apprenticeship but is not yet a master craftsman.

In the meantime, Benjamin needed a place to live. He had been staying with Andrew Bradford, but Keimer did not want his employee to live with a competitor. Benjamin was able to rent a room in John Read's house, writing in his *Autobiography* that he was now able to make "rather a more respectable appearance in the eyes of Miss Read than I had done when she first happen'd to see me eating my roll in the street."

Philadelphia was not a large city at the time. Its population of 6,000 was just half that of Boston. Benjamin was tall, handsome, and intelligent and possessed a genial, outgoing personality. He soon became well known and well liked by almost everyone, even the governor of Pennsylvania, Sir William Keith.

Keith, who did not think highly of either Keimer or Andrew Bradford, had been shown a letter written by Benjamin. Keith was so impressed with its language that he thought Benjamin should have a printing business of his own. Keith appeared at Keimer's door one day, and the printer was stunned to find out that the governor was there to see his young helper.

At a nearby tavern over a glass of wine, Keith suggested that Benjamin go to Boston, armed with a letter from the governor, to see if he could get enough money from his father to open his own business. Keith promised to give Benjamin all government printing contracts once he had set up shop.

TO BOSTON

In April 1724, Franklin sailed to Boston, dropping in on his surprised family after an absence of seven months. All were glad to see him, except for his brother James. He looked at his former apprentice, who was wearing an expensive new suit, and returned silently to his work.

Josiah Franklin was impressed with Benjamin's new status and Governor Keith's letter. He did not, however, come up with the necessary money. He thought Benjamin too young at 18 to run his own business and had debts of his own. He told Benjamin to return to Philadelphia and promised that if Benjamin saved close to the necessary amount by the time he was 21, he would advance him the rest.

Franklin returned to Philadelphia discouraged. But Keith did not give up on him. If Franklin's father would not set him up, the governor would do it himself. He told Franklin to go to London where he could use letters of credit supplied by Keith to buy everything needed.

The next ship from Philadelphia to London did not sail until November. Franklin kept his plans to himself, continuing to work for Keimer and saving as much money as possible. He also used the time to court his landlady's daughter, asking her mother for Deborah Read's hand in marriage because her father had since died. Mrs. Read liked Franklin, as did most people, but she said that he was too young, not yet in business, and about to go off to England, so the marriage would have to wait until he returned.

When Franklin boarded the *London Hope* on November 5, 1724, he did so not only without a wife but also without Governor Keith's letters of credit. He had been told repeatedly that they would be ready in time for his trip. Just before the ship sailed, Franklin tried once more and was told that the letters would be delivered to him on the

Franklin found himself well suited to printing. This printing press, circa 1720, was used by Franklin in England in 1726 and is now housed in the National Museum of American History, in Washington, D.C.

ship. Later, when he questioned the ship's captain, he was told that all letters were in a sack in storage and that Franklin could get them just before arrival.

Before the ship docked, the captain allowed Franklin to go through the bag. There were no letters for him from Keith. He explained his predicament to Thomas Denham, a Philadelphia merchant with whom he had struck up a friendship on the ship. Denham, according to his *Autobiography*, "laughed at the notion of the governor's giving me a letter of credit, having, as he said, no credit to give." Denham told Franklin that Keith was notorious for making promises he had no intention of keeping. He advised Franklin to seek employment with a London printer to earn money and increase his skills.

LONDON

Franklin followed the advice, finding work at Samuel Palmer's printing business. While there, he wrote and printed an essay titled "A Dissertation on Liberty and Necessity, Pleasure and Pain." In it, he rejected the strict creed under which he had been raised; that every person is preordained by God to either damnation or salvation. Rather, he wrote, there is good in every person, and all "must be equally esteemed by the creator." He was moving toward the philosophy that eventually guided his life, that one's highest calling was not faith in a supernatural being, but doing good for one's neighbors and the community.

Franklin and a friend, James Ralph, roomed together and enjoyed London's delights. Ralph was unable to find work, and it was mostly Franklin's earnings that were spent, according to his *Autobiography*, in "going to plays and other places of amusement." The memory of Deborah Read grew dimmer. Franklin wrote to her only once during the 21 months he spent in England, and that was to tell her he was not coming home anytime soon. He later made advances to a young woman with whom Ralph was living, which ended their friendship.

After about a year at Palmer's, Franklin took a job at Watts, a far larger printing house. He began as a press operator, but he soon showed his skill in composing type and was promoted. He was known as the Water American by his fellow printers who, he wrote in his *Autobiography*, were "great guzzlers of beer," while Franklin drank mostly water to save money and keep his head clear.

He was also known for his physical strength. He wrote with some pride in his *Autobiography* that he was able to climb stairs with a heavy form of lead type in each hand while his colleagues could barely manage one form with both hands.

He took up swimming once more and so impressed some of his friends that one of them offered to help him set up a swimming school. Another offer, however, was more appealing. His friend Denham was going to open a general store in Philadelphia and offered Franklin a position as his clerk. Franklin accepted, and they sailed for America in July 1726.

On the voyage, Franklin drew up one of his many personal improvement plans. It contained four basic rules: to be frugal [thrifty] until he was out of debt, to try to speak the truth and give no one false hopes, to apply himself to business and not be lured by get-rich-quick schemes, and to never speak ill of anyone. All these sprang from personal experience, and it was typical of Franklin to examine his shortcomings candidly and seek to remedy them.

BACK TO PRINTING

Denham opened his store in the autumn of 1726, but Franklin, although writing in his *Autobiography* that he became an "expert in selling," also referred to it as "disagreeable work." It did not last long. Franklin and Denham both contracted pleurisy, a disease of the lungs, early in 1727. Franklin recovered, but Denham did not, and he died in 1728. Denham had been forced to close the store, which meant Franklin had to return to work for Keimer.

Keimer did not particularly like Franklin, whom he felt had deserted him, but needed his skills to help print currency for the colony of New Jersey. He also needed Franklin to train four young apprentices, intending to dispense him after the training was done.

At one point, Franklin quit and walked out, asking one of the apprentices, Hugh Meredith, to bring his belongings to where he was living. Meredith arrived with Franklin's belongings and a proposition. His own apprenticeship would soon be done, and his father, who admired Franklin and hoped his influence would curb Meredith's drinking problem, had agreed to loan them the money to set up their own shop. Franklin agreed, gave Meredith's father a list of needed supplies, and went back to Keimer's for the time left in Meredith's apprenticeship.

The equipment Franklin had purchased from England arrived at the end of May in 1728. Meredith's apprenticeship was completed two weeks later. Both he and Franklin then left Keimer's employment on good terms. They did not tell their employer that they planned to set up a rival shop.

Franklin and Meredith rented a three-story house on Market Street. They had barely finished setting up the equipment when they had their first customer, a man from the countryside who had just arrived in the city and was looking for a printer. The job—exactly what it was is not known—brought a payment of five shillings that, Franklin wrote in his *Autobiography*, "gave me more pleasure than any [golden] crown I have since earned." At age 22, the one-time runaway who had landed in Philadelphia only five years earlier was the proprietor of his own business. Before very long, he would also become a successful businessman and the most widely read American author of his day.

2

Printer and Publisher

In 1728, at the age of 22, Benjamin Franklin had his own printing business. Within five years he also had his own newspaper, magazine, and an almanac that was to become one of the most frequently read and best-loved pieces of American literature. Through a combination of hard work, humor, and shrewdness, Franklin would grow wealthy enough to retire from business and pursue even greater goals.

Franklin and Meredith's second printing job was much larger than the first. It was a 178-page history of the Society of Friends, or the Quakers. To meet the deadline, Franklin worked late into each night. According to J.A. Leo Lemay's *The Life of Benjamin Franklin*, Franklin quoted a neighbor as saying, "I see him still at work when I go home from Club; and he is at Work about before his Neighbours are out of bed."

Franklin knew that more money was to be made from publishing than from printing alone. He decided to start a newspaper to compete with one published by Andrew Bradford, but he made the mistake of telling a friend who in turn told Samuel Keimer. Keimer promptly started a paper of his own, the *Pennsylvania Gazette.*

Franklin knew that there was no room in Philadelphia for a third newspaper, so he set out to make Bradford's dull *American Weekly Mercury* so successful that it would put Keimer's paper out of business. To do this, Franklin invented another personality similar to Silence Dogood—the Busy Body, America's first gossip columnist.

THE BUSY BODY

Aided by his friend Joseph Breintnall, Franklin wrote a series of essays in which the Busy Body promised, as quoted by Walter Isaacson, to "take nobody's business wholly into my own hands." Furthermore, he wrote, "If any are offended at my exposing their private vices, I promise they shall have the satisfaction, in a very little time, of seeing their good friends and neighbors in the same circumstances."

As it turned out, the Busy Body did not engage in spicy gossip to any great extent, preferring to make fun in general of people who did things such as spoil their children or fall for get-rich-quick schemes. He also ridiculed some of Pennsylvania's wealthiest men for being too class conscious, but he did not reveal their names.

He also took on, for the first time, the Penn family, who owned the Pennsylvania colony. The issue was paper currency, favored by merchants and tradesmen such as Franklin but not by the large landowners, who preferred hard currency such as gold and silver. A greater money supply provided by paper currency, the Busy Body argued, would lower interest rates and encourage more trade. Franklin was no doubt sincere in his beliefs, but he had another reason to support paper currency. He wanted to be the one to print it.

Franklin enjoyed enormous success as a printer. He did so well that he was able to retire from the business and pursue other interests.

The Busy Body accomplished his mission. Keimer went into debt and moved to the island of Barbados in the Caribbean. Before he left, however, he sold the *Pennsylvania Gazette* to Franklin and Meredith to help pay his debts. The October 2, 1729, edition of the *Gazette* carried the names of the new publishers. It also got in a dig at both Keimer and Bradford by saying, as quoted by J.A. Leo Lemay in *The Life of Benjamin Franklin*, "many people have long desired to see a good News-Paper in Pennsylvania."

And the *Gazette* was a good newspaper. Talcott Williams, former dean of the Columbia University journalism school, said

Franklin "was the inventor of newspaper English, direct, immediate, knowing humor as well as argument, using the speech of the people," according to Lemay. While the other six colonial newspapers filled their pages with news from abroad, lists of ships' passengers, government documents, and even articles from encyclopedias, the *Gazette* featured crime news, obituaries (which were rare at the time), humorous yet sharply pointed essays, and even a sex and morals column.

Franklin was not an editor like Bradford, who was content to avoid controversy and follow the party line laid down by the colony's ruling class. He also was not a passionate crusader like his brother James. Franklin was somewhere in the middle, interested in watching those on both sides of a question and occasionally taking sides. Yet even when he took a strong stand, Franklin would just as likely as not come up with an ironic quip about his own depth of feeling.

PROSPERITY

The newspaper's circulation grew and the business prospered. In 1730 Franklin and Meredith's firm was named the official printer for the Pennsylvania Assembly. Bradford had previously held the contract for this work, but he did a sloppy job printing a speech by the governor. Franklin printed the same speech as elegantly as possible and sent it to his connections in the assembly. "It strengthened the hands of our friends in the House," he wrote in his *Autobiography*, referring in general to those who opposed the Penn family, "and they voted us their printers."

The road to prosperity was not entirely smooth. Hugh Meredith had not stopped drinking to excess as his father had hoped, and the operation of the entire business fell to Franklin. Even worse, Meredith's father had paid only half the money due for the equipment—about 100 British pounds—and did not have the rest. The merchant who was owed the money threatened a lawsuit that, if successful, would have put Franklin out of business.

Two of Franklin's friends, William Coleman and Robert Grace, offered to loan him the necessary funds on one condition: Franklin had to drop Hugh Meredith as a partner. Franklin, however, felt indebted to the Merediths and offered to surrender the entire business to them if they assumed full responsibility for the debt. Hugh Meredith declined, saying he was not cut out to be a printer. He said that if Franklin would repay his father what had been spent on the equipment, assume all the debt, and pay some of Meredith's personal debts, he would dissolve the partnership.

Franklin accepted, borrowed money from his friends, and became sole proprietor of the business. In his *Autobiography*, Franklin called Coleman and Grace "two true friends, whose kindness I have never forgotten, nor ever shall forget while I can remember any thing."

MARRIAGE

With his business thus secured, Franklin decided it was time to marry, as was expected of an up-and-coming businessman in Philadelphia. He turned to the first girl he had seen in Philadelphia seven years earlier, Deborah Read. While Franklin had been in England, Deborah had married John Rogers, who abandoned her about a year later and, deeply in debt, fled to the West Indies. As Franklin wrote in his *Autobiography*, "our mutual affection was revived, but now there were great objections to our union." For one, Rogers had been reported dead but there was no confirmation. If he was alive, Deborah would still be legally married and guilty of bigamy if she married Franklin. Marriage with Deborah might then also open Franklin to lawsuits by those to whom Rogers owed money.

The couple got around the difficulty in September of 1730 by entering into a common-law marriage. They lived as man and wife

"ON CONVERSATION"

Franklin wrote an article titled "On Conversation," which emphasized the importance in discussion of conceding to the other person's opinion, or at least appearing to concede. "Would you win the hearts of others, you must not seem to vie with them, but to admire them. Give them every opportunity of displaying their own qualifications, and when you have indulged their vanity, they will praise you in turn and prefer you above others. . . . Such is the vanity of mankind that minding what others say is a much surer way of pleasing them than talking well ourselves."

The article included a list, in order of gravity, of the sins one could commit during a conversation. First and most important, he wrote, is "talking overmuch." He painted a verbal picture of two such marathon talkers vying with one another, who "stare and interrupt one another at every turn, and watch with utmost impatience for a cough or pause, when they may crowd a word in edgewise."

Other conversational sins included seeming bored; talking about oneself; prying into the other's personal life; telling long and boring stories, something Franklin thought old people were particularly guilty of; contradicting the other person; belittling the other's views; and spreading gossip. The quotations are from *Benjamin Franklin: An American Life,* by Walter Isaacson.

but no formal ceremony took place. The marriage may not have been passionate, but Franklin and Deborah were genuinely affectionate toward each other, as their later letters show. In his *Autobiography,* Franklin called her "a good and faithful helpmate, assisted me much by attending the shop" and added that they "have ever mutually endeavored to make each other happy."

Another "great objection" to the marriage was Franklin's illegitimate son, William. The date of William's birth is uncertain but seems to have been either a few months before or a few months after his father's marriage. The identity of the mother is even more of a mystery. Franklin wrote in his *Autobiography* about his "intrigues with low women," but it seems unlikely that he would acknowledge a child born to a prostitute. Some historians have speculated that Deborah was the mother, but letters written much later by family members indicate that she disliked William and included him in the family only for Benjamin's sake.

It was not too long before the Franklins had a child of their own. Francis Franklin, called Franky by his parents, was born in 1732 but died of smallpox at the age of four. His death seems to be one of the few events that affected Franklin deeply. The memory was so painful that he could not write about it in his *Autobiography*. It would be 1743 before the couple's only other child, Sarah, nicknamed Sally, was born.

POOR RICHARD'S ALMANACK

In the interval between the births of Franklin's children, his business grew steadily. Much of the growth was due to the publication of what was to be not only Franklin's best-selling work, but also his most famous. This work, *Poor Richard's Almanack,* is a cornerstone of American literature.

If an American household at the time contained at least two books, they were likely to be the Bible and an almanac. Indeed, almanacs outsold Bibles because a new one had to be purchased each year. Almanacs contained tables of phases of the moon and positions of the stars, information used by many farmers as guides for when to plant and harvest. They had charts of tides, which were indispensible to sailors. They listed days on which courts would convene, markets would open, and fairs would be held.

In 1732, there were six almanacs in Philadelphia, two of them printed, but not written, by Franklin. But when both authors later took their business to Andrew Bradford, Franklin decided to start an almanac of his own. He took the name Poor Richard by combining that of a popular English almanac writer of the previous century, Richard Sanders, with *Poor Robert's Almanack*, which had been published by his brother James.

As usual, however, Franklin brought his own special style. Writing as Poor Richard, his shrewish wife Bridget, and other characters, Franklin spiced up the almanac with essays in which these common folk poked fun at the stuffiness of the upper classes. In so doing, wrote historian Alan Taylor as quoted by Isaacson, Franklin influenced "a long line of humorists—from Davy Crockett and Mark Twain to Garrison Keillor [who] still rework the prototypes [characters] created by Franklin."

Poor Richard's Almanack, however, is best known for its aphorisms, or short sayings designed to convey a moral truth. Such timeless maxims as "A penny saved is a penny earned," "God helps those who help themselves," and "Early to bed and early to rise makes a man healthy, wealthy, and wise" are all to be found there. Other favorites include "Haste makes waste," "Eat to live, and not live to eat," and "Diligence is the mother of good luck."

Poor Richard's sayings were by no means all original. Franklin used many time-tested proverbs, some of them going back to Aesop's Fables. Franklin freely admitted this in his *Autobiography*, writing that "not a tenth part of the wisdom was my own." He did, however, give old sayings a new twist. "Many strokes fell great trees" became "Little strokes fell great oaks." "Fresh fish and new-come guests smell, but that they are three days old" was turned into "Fish and visitors stink in three days."

Poor Richard's Almanack was a phenomenal success, selling an average of about 10,000 copies annually over its 25 years of publication.

Poor Richard, 1739.

AN

Almanack

For the Year of Christ

1739,

Being the Third after LEAP YEAR.

And makes since the Creation	Years
By the Account of the Eastern *Greeks*	7247
By the Latin Church, when ⊙ ent. ♈	6938
By the Computation of *W. W.*	5748
By the *Roman* Chronology	5688
By the *Jewish* Rabbies	5500

Wherein is contained,

The Lunations, Eclipses, Judgment of the Weather, Spring Tides, Planets Motions & mutual Aspects, Sun and Moon's Rising and Setting, Length of Days, Time of High Water, Fairs, Courts, and observable Days.

Fitted to the Latitude of Forty Degrees, and a Meridian of Five Hours West from *London*, but may without sensible Error, serve all the adjacent Places, even from *Newfoundland* to *South-Carolina.*

By *RICHARD SAUNDERS*, Philom.

PHILADELPHIA:
Printed and sold by *B. FRANKLIN*, at the New Printing-Office near the Market.

Franklin's wry style and use of fictional characters added to the popularity of *Poor Richard's Almanack*. One of the most popular almanacs in the colonies, it was published for 25 years.

Its success reached far beyond Pennsylvania and even beyond the colonies. The final edition, published in 1757, was reprinted in 145 editions and in 7 languages. In that edition, Franklin assembled all his aphorisms on frugality and put them in the mouth of one Father Abraham lecturing a crowd. As quoted by Isaacson, the article's ending was pure Franklin when, from the back of the crowd, Poor Richard said, "The people heard it and approved the doctrine, and immediately practiced the contrary."

THE PERFECTION PLAN

Franklin, however, did practice what he preached, or at least made a determined effort to do so. He set out an ambitious plan to achieve what he called in his *Autobiography* "moral perfection." He drew up a list of 12 virtues he thought necessary to gain such perfection: temperance (moderation in food and drink); silence; order; resolution (completing tasks); frugality; industry; sincerity; justice; moderation (avoiding extremes of temper); cleanliness; tranquility; and chastity. When a friend pointed out that Franklin was often guilty of pride, he added a thirteenth virtue—humility.

To keep track of his progress, Franklin devised a chart with a row for each virtue and a column for each day of the week. Each night he reviewed his day, placing marks in the appropriate box to indicate where he had fallen short. "I was surprised," he wrote in his *Autobiography*, "to find myself so much fuller of faults than I had imagined."

The virtue that gave him the most trouble was order. He confessed in his *Autobiography* that he was careless "with regard to places for things, papers, etc." Also, predictably, he fell short in overcoming pride. He was quick to acknowledge this weakness and wrote that "even if I could conceive that I had compleatly overcome it, I should probably be proud of my humility."

Franklin's moral perfection project was plain and practical. The virtues were those that he thought could best be applied to ordinary people. Qualities such as valor or nobility were omitted. So, too, were piety and devotion. But Franklin's virtues did have a religious basis, which he set forth in 1728 in a paper written for his private use titled "Articles of Belief and Acts of Religion."

The paper began with a forthright statement: "I believe there is one Supreme most perfect Being." He then set out four options for what God might be: one who had predetermined everything at the time of creation; one who allowed matters to proceed on their own and never interferes; one who predetermined some things but allows others to proceed on their own and never interferes; and one who "sometimes interferes by His particular providence." Franklin chose the last option, reasoning that any of the first three would mean that God is not supreme and all-powerful.

Such a God, he wrote, is so far above humanity as to have no need of prayers or praise. Nevertheless, he thought that it did people good to "pray for Him for His favor and protection." But more pleasing to God than prayer, Franklin wrote, is virtue. In his view, therefore, the best way for people to praise God and be thankful was to lead a virtuous life, being kind and doing good for others. In a 1738 letter to his parents, quoted by Isaacson, Franklin said that people will be judged by God "not . . . by what we *thought*, but by what we *did*."

POSTMASTER

Such lofty sentiments did not keep Franklin from being a hard-headed businessman. Even though his newspaper was of higher quality than Bradford's, his rival had the advantage of being postmaster of Philadelphia. As such, he sent his own paper through the mail but refused to send Franklin's. So Franklin had to bribe postal riders to get distribution. But when Bradford's bookkeeping was questioned, Franklin convinced Alexander Spotswood, postmaster for all the colonies, to oust Bradford and give him the Philadelphia post. The increased circulation and advertising, Franklin wrote in his *Autobiography*, "came to afford me a considerable income."

Franklin tried to make that income even more considerable with the publication of his *General Magazine* in 1740, but it was not a success. A magazine, at that time, was a collection of articles, essays, and poems that had already been published elsewhere, something like *Reader's Digest*. There simply were not enough good sources of material in America. The publication lasted only a few months.

Other ventures, however, were more successful. Franklin printed Bibles, which always sold well, and the first novel published in America, a reprint of Samuel Richardson's *Pamela*. Franklin also established printers in other colonies and formed partnerships with existing printers.

The money from such ventures, plus income from property he had purchased in Philadelphia, made Franklin a rich man. Wealth, however, was not his ambition. As quoted in Ronald Clark's *Benjamin Franklin*, he wrote to his mother that when he died, "I would rather have it said, 'He lived usefully,' than 'He died rich.'"

On January 1, 1748, he went into partnership with his foreman, David Hall, and retired from his active role in the business. He continued to receive half the profits. He would now, he wrote to a friend, as quoted by H.W. Brands, have time to "read, study, make experiments, and converse at large with such ingenious and worthy men as are pleased to honor me with their friendship or acquaintance, on such points as may produce something for the common benefit of mankind, uninterrupted by business." Franklin's experiments would, indeed, benefit humanity, and they would earn him a high place among ingenious and worthy men.

3

Inventor

Franklin once wrote that, while it is useful to know that fine china will fall and break if not supported, it is not necessary to understand the underlying natural laws. "It is a pleasure indeed to know them," he wrote, as quoted by Walter Isaacson, "but we can preserve our china without it." While he was intensely curious in *why*, Franklin was much more interested in *how* and, moreover, in putting *how* to practical use.

Franklin's interest in cause, effect, and practical application was lifelong. It showed up early when he rigged up a kite to act as a sail, pulling him along as he floated in Boston's Charles River. As a teenager in his brother's print shop, he became interested in lead poisoning and later made it the subject of Philadelphia's first locally written medical paper. At 20, instead of relaxing on the deck of the ship carrying him home from England, he collected seaweed and made a detailed study of the tiny crabs he found there. On another occasion he conducted an experiment showing that ants could communicate.

Franklin was also interested in how different colors absorbed the sun's heat. He experimented by laying squares of colored cloth on snow and measuring the rate of melting. He observed that dark colors absorbed more heat and suggested that people should wear light-colored clothing in the summer and that fruit storage sheds should be painted black in the winter to retain heat.

Another question he investigated was why ship voyages from America to England usually took less time than a return trip. Sailors had known for centuries about an ocean current that swept up the eastern side of North America and then northeast to Britain, but no one had mapped it. Franklin enlisted a cousin, whaling ship captain Timothy Folger, to map the current so that ships could take advantage of it sailing east and avoid it coming west. In 1762 Franklin named the current the Gulf Stream.

THE TINKERER

Such projects, however, even if they had practical applications, were mostly intellectual exercises. What Franklin really enjoyed was taking tools in hand to turn ideas into useful items.

Much of Franklin's tinkering involved the tools of the printing trade. People had been making prints of leaves by covering them with a light coat of ink and pressing them against paper for many years. Franklin devised a method of pressing a leaf into a soft substance to create an impression. He then made a lead plate of the impression to use on a printing press. As usual, there was a practical application: Paper currency bearing such imprints was almost impossible to counterfeit.

Franklin was among the first to suggest that printing onto pottery or tile might be possible. He also brought about a fundamental change in the way printing presses were made that caused less wear on the parts. He also experimented with paper, using the mineral mica to strengthen the type used in printing currency, even though longer-lasting paper meant less work for a printer.

Another project, the Franklin stove, has survived in various forms to the present day. Stoves were a part of every colonial household. They were used both for cooking and heating. Franklin was convinced that they could be made more efficient. Most produced too much smoke and too little heat and used far too much wood. In a promotional pamphlet of 1744 quoted by H.W. Brands, Franklin wrote that wood that "might be had at every man's door, must now be fetched 100 miles to some towns."

THE FRANKLIN STOVE

Franklin began experimenting with a new stove in January 1737. He bought a stove and a quantity of steel from a Philadelphia merchant and went to work. Once Franklin perfected the design he bought more stoves, modified them, and started selling them to his friends.

The stove worked on the principle of convection, the transfer of heat by means of circulating a heated substance, in this case air. A false back was built into a brick fireplace and the iron stove placed inside. A shutter door on the front of the stove regulated the wood fire built inside.

The heat and smoke rose up at the rear of the stove, over the top of an air box, down the back of the air box, and then beneath the false fireplace back and up the chimney. The air box received fresh air through an opening at the bottom. This air was warmed by the heat surrounding the box and then went through sets of louvers, or narrow openings, on each side of the stove into the room.

In 1741 Franklin went into partnership with Robert Grace, one of the two men who had saved Franklin's printing business years before and who owned an iron foundry. At first, the Pennsylvania Fireplaces, as Franklin called them, were sold mostly to his friends. By 1744, however, they were being manufactured in two sizes and marketed throughout the northeastern colonies by friends and family members.

Franklin's pamphlet describing the stove's virtues, as quoted by J.A. Leo Lemay, was a masterpiece of advertising. Unlike some enclosed iron stoves, he wrote, the door on the front gave occupants a view of the fire, "which in itself is a pleasant Thing." The room would be made "twice as warm as it used to be, with a quarter of the Wood." There was an appeal to cooks in that dishes could be kept warm by placing them on top of the stove. He even hinted that women would be kept looking younger since the smoke released into rooms by other stoves "do very much contribute to damage the Eyes, dry and shrivel the Skin, and bring on early the Appearances of Old Age."

Sales of the Pennsylvania Fireplaces were brisk throughout New England and the Mid-Atlantic colonies. One customer gave the stove its eventual name, writing to the *Boston Evening Post*, as quoted by Isaacson, that the stoves "ought to be called, both in justice and gratitude, Mr. Franklin's stoves. I believe all who have experienced the comfort and benefit of them will join with me that the author of this happy invention merits a statue." Franklin stoves are still sold under that name.

The deputy governor of Pennsylvania was so pleased with the stove that he offered to give Franklin a patent on its manufacture. Franklin refused. He explained in his *Autobiography* that, "as we enjoy great Advantages from the Inventions of others, we should be glad of an Opportunity to serve others by any Invention of ours, and this we should do freely and generously." Years later he was disturbed to learn that a London manufacturer had made some minor adjustments to the design, took out a patent, "and made as I was told a little Fortune by it."

ELECTRICITY

Most of Franklin's fame as a scientist and inventor, however, rests on his famous experiments with electricity. Scientists had recognized electricity as a natural force since ancient times, but no one knew what caused it or how to harness its power. It was mostly used for amusement, creating sparks or making a person's hair stand on end.

FRANKLIN AND TURKEYS

Franklin had a high regard for wild turkeys and even included them in some of his electrical experiments. He wanted to understand the amount of harm done to living things by increasingly strong currents of electricity. In about 1749 he started performing such experiments on birds.

Chickens, he wrote, were easily killed with the current from a single Leyden jar, but that a turkey "though thrown into violent conventions, and then lying as dead for some minutes, would recover in less than a quarter of an hour." But by hooking up several jars in sequence, "we killed a turkey with them of about 10 lb. weight and suppose they would have killed a much larger."

Ever seeking a practical outcome, Franklin added, "I conceit that the birds killed in this manner eat uncommonly tender."

Much later, in 1784, he wrote to his daughter that the turkey, and not the bald eagle, should be the national bird. H.W. Brands included the letter in *The First American: The Life and Times of Benjamin Franklin*.

It was just such an entertainment that attracted Franklin. In 1743, he attended a performance in Boston by Dr. Archibald Spencer, who did tricks with static electricity generated by a spinning glass tube. Spencer later came to Philadelphia, where Franklin acted as his agent, advertising his performances and selling tickets.

Franklin became more and more fascinated by electricity. In 1747, shortly before Spencer returned to England, Franklin bought all of his equipment so he could conduct experiments on his own. He soon wrote to Peter Collinson, a London bookseller, as quoted

[The eagle] is a Bird of bad moral Character. He does not get his Living honestly. You may have seen him perched on some dead Tree near the River, where, too lazy to fish for himself, he watches the Labour of the Fishing Hawk; and when that diligent Bird has at length taken a Fish, and is bearing it to his Nest for the Support of his Mate and young Ones, the Bald Eagle pursues him and takes it from him . . .

He is therefore by no means a proper Emblem for the brave and honest Cincinnati [a proposed order of former soldiers] of America who have driven all the King birds from our Country . . .

I am on this account not displeased that the Figure is not known as a Bald Eagle, but looks more like a Turkey. For the Truth the Turkey is in Comparison a much more respectable Bird, and withal a true original Native of America. . . . He is besides, though a little vain and silly, a Bird of Courage, and would not hesitate to attack a Grenadier of the British Guards who should presume to invade his Farm Yard with a red Coat on.

by Brands, "I was never before engaged in any study that so totally engrossed my attention and my time."

He found that if a person touched the glass tube, then let go of the tube to touch another person, a spark would result. From this he deduced that electricity was not only generated but also collected until discharged. As quoted by Isaacson, he wrote to Collinson that the person initially receiving the charge was "electrised positively" and the person to whom the charge was passed was "electrised negatively." He added that "these terms we may use until your philosophers give us better." No one did, and "positive" and "negative" remain basic terms in electricity.

In discovering the principle of positive and negative charges, Franklin did away with the old notion that there were two kinds of electricity, called vitreous and resinous. He showed that there was only one kind, and that a positive charge was always offset by a negative charge. The discovery of this concept, known as conservation of charge, was called by Harvard Professor I. Bernard Cohen, as quoted by Isaacson, "of the same fundamental importance to physical science as Newton's law of conservation of energy."

Positive and *negative* were not the only terms originated by Franklin that would become part of the standard language of electricity. He put names to electrical concepts such as *charge, neutral,* and *conductor.* When he began to use a new method of storing electricity, the Leyden jar, he discovered that by wiring several jars together he could produce a stronger current. He named this device after the military term for multiple artillery pieces acting in combination—a battery.

THE LIGHTNING ROD

Franklin noted that a person touching a positively charged glass tube could attract the charge. He began experimenting to see what else could do so, and thus made one of his most important discoveries. He

Once out of the printing business, Franklin was free to make other important contributions to America, including his inventions and science experiments. Franklin used this vacuum pump to conduct experiments with electricity.

found that a metal rod, preferably a pointed one, could draw a charge from an electrified object. Furthermore, if the rod was grounded, or linked to the ground by either a person or a wire, the charge would pass through into the earth.

Franklin was intrigued by the possibilities. He and many others had noted the similarities between electrical sparks and lightning, such as crooked direction, bright light, and a crackling sound, but no one had proved that lighting was a form of electricity. If it was, he wrote to Collinson, as quoted by Brands, then perhaps through the use of such metal rods "houses, ships, even towns and churches may be effectually secured from the stroke of lightning."

First, however, it had to be proved that lightning was, indeed, electricity. In his 1749 journal, quoted by Ronald Clark, Franklin issued the call to action: "Let the experiment be made." In a 1750 letter to Collinson quoted by Brands, he outlined the way it should be done: At a time when lightning was in the area, a man should stand in a high tower or steeple from which a pointed iron rod 20 to 30 feet long would extend upward. Then, "the man . . . might be electrified and afford sparks, the rod drawing fire to him from the cloud." There should be no danger to the man, he wrote, if he stands in a clean, dry place and thus is not grounded. To make certain, however, the man could hold, with insulated handles, a metal wire that could be touched to the base of the rod to draw off the electrical charge.

Franklin would not be the first to conduct such an experiment. Collinson presented his letters to the prestigious academy of science in London known as the Royal Society and they were widely published. Soon afterward, they were translated into French and were read with enthusiasm by King Louis XV, who urged his own scientists to conduct Franklin's proposed experiment. So, on May 10, 1752, just outside Paris, a retired soldier volunteered to stand in a sentry box with a 40-foot iron rod. When a storm cloud passed overhead, the soldier picked up a wire that had been insulated with a glass bottle. When he held the wire to the rod, sparks flew and there was a loud sizzling sound accompanied by a smell of sulfur.

Lightning and the smell it sometimes created had long been associated by many people with the devil. The soldier, frightened, called out for the local priest, who stood in the crowd nearby. The priest grabbed the bottle and touched the wire to the rod six more times, producing the same result. There was no doubt now that lightning and electricity were the same. French scientist Thomas-François Dalibard wrote to the French Royal Academy of Sciences, as quoted by Clark, "M. Franklin's idea has ceased to be a conjecture . . . here it has become a reality."

THE KITE EXPERIMENT

It became a reality for Franklin the next month as a result of his famous kite experiment. For some reason, he did not describe the experiment in his *Autobiography*. The best description was given by the English physicist Joseph Priestly, with whom Franklin later frequently corresponded.

According to Priestly, Franklin delayed conducting an experiment of his own because he was waiting for a Philadelphia church to complete a steeple that he thought would be suitable. He grew tired of waiting, however, and hit on the idea of flying a kite with a sharp wire extending from the top during a storm. Franklin reasoned that the wire would attract an electrical charge, which would then travel down the wet string and collect in a key tied to the end.

Dreading the ridicule that might come his way should the experiment fail, he was accompanied only by his son, William, who was then about 21 years old and not the small boy portrayed in some famous paintings of the event. Several thunderclouds passed overhead with no results, and he was at the point of giving up when,

Franklin's 1752 kite experiment, which proved to him that lightning was an electrical force, brought him fame throughout the colonies.

Priestly wrote as quoted by Clark, "he observed some loose threads of the hempen string to stand erect, and to avoid one another, just as if they had been suspended on a common conductor. Struck with this promising appearance, he immediately presented his knuckle to the key, and . . . the discovery was complete. . . . This happened in June 1752, a month after the electricians in France had verified the same theory, but before he heard of anything they had done."

Before long, lightning rods were being installed throughout the colonies and Europe. Franklin took pride, evident in his *Autobiography*, that "my book (a pamphlet made from his letters to Callison) was translated into the Italian, German, and Latin languages; and the doctrine it contain'd was by degrees universally adopted by the philosophers of Europe." He became the most famous of all Americans at the time, subsequently being elected to the Royal Society and receiving its Copley Medal for scientific achievement. Yale and Harvard, which he had mocked while writing as Silence Dogood, gave him honorary degrees.

Franklin's interest in scientific phenomena would continue through his later career as a politician and statesman. In his eighties he was still investigating the Gulf Stream, wrote a 40-page paper on the design of ships' hulls and other things dealing with sailing, and experimented on ways to fix smoky chimneys, and, when he was no longer able to climb stairs or a ladder, he invented a mechanical arm for taking books from a shelf. As always, his research and experiments were designed not to reveal the truth of some natural law, but to make something useful. As Poor Richard put it, "An investment in knowledge always pays the best interest."

4

Public Citizen

Benjamin Franklin established the Library Company of Philadelphia in 1731, giving it the Latin motto *Communiter Bona profundere Deum est,* or "To pour forth benefits for the common good is divine." It could just as easily have been a motto for Franklin himself. His long history of community service projects exemplifies his belief that serving God means serving one's neighbors.

It was not a solitary undertaking. The most sociable of men, Franklin loved meeting with people, but he believed that there should be a purpose to such gatherings. This tendency to form associations for the common good was seen as uniquely American by some European observers. "Franklin epitomized the Rotarian urge," writes Isaacson, "and has remained, after more than two centuries, a symbol of it."

His first such undertaking occurred in 1727 shortly after his return from London. He formed a club of 12 young tradesmen like himself. Its formal name was the Junto, but it was known unofficially as the Leather Apron Club, a reference to the working-class status of the members.

Each Friday night, according to his *Autobiograpy*, "every member, in his turn, should produce one or more queries on any point of Morals, Politics, or Natural Philosophy, to be discuss'd by the company; and once in three months produce and read an essay of his own writing, on any subject he pleased." Debates were to be "conducted in the sincere spirit of inquiry after truth, without fondness for dispute, or desire of victory."

Franklin joined in these debates, but not with the vigor that he might have. He was aware of his fondness for talking and worried in his *Autobiography* that it "only made me acceptable to trifling company." He resolved to acquire knowledge "rather by the use of the ear than of the tongue."

The Junto existed not only for mutual education, but also for the kind of mutual benefit that would later be called networking. The members included Hugh Meredith, Franklin's business partner; Joseph Breintnall, who helped write the Busy Body essays; Thomas Godfrey, whose family roomed in Franklin's house; and William Coleman and Robert Grace, who would later help Franklin financially.

The Junto first met in a tavern, but as members prospered the group was able to rent a house. More men wanted to join, but Franklin thought the number should stay at about a dozen. Rather, he urged each member to form new clubs of their own so that the benefits could spread far beyond the original group.

THE LIBRARY

The Junto met continuously until 1765, and by that time, according to Lemay, "had touched and improved nearly every life in Philadelphia."

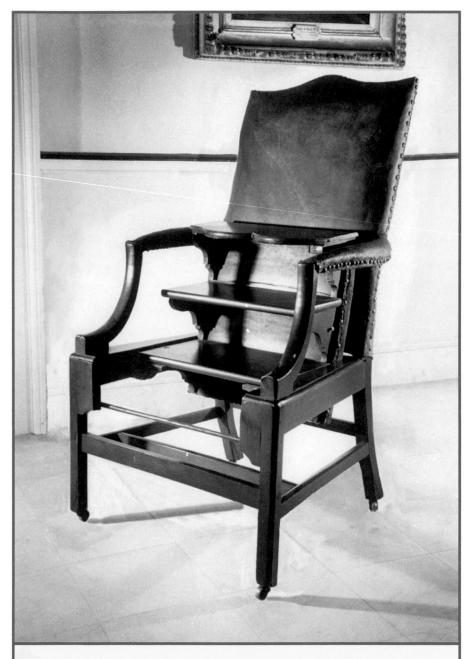

With the Library Company of Philadelphia, Franklin created the first subscription library in America. This chair, which converts to a stepladder, was designed by Franklin for use in the library.

A major reason for its impact was that Franklin used it as a platform from which to launch most of his civic projects. The first of these was the formation of a library.

Franklin first proposed that the Junto members pool their books for use by all. There proved to be too few books calling for too much care, and the collection was disbanded after a year. Franklin then proposed to create a subscription library, the first in America. The idea was that people would put up an initial fee of 40 shillings—about $320 in current U.S. dollars—and pay 10 shillings a year for 50 years. This money would be used to buy books, mostly from England, to stock a library for use by subscribers.

At first, Franklin found few takers and thought perhaps it was because people thought that he, as the person who had the original idea, was trying to improve his own reputation in the community. And so, his *Autobiography* states, "I therefore put myself as much as I could out of sight, and stated it as a scheme of a number of friends, who had requested me to go about and propose it to such as they thought lovers of reading."

His tactic worked. With the help of Junto members, he was able to find 40 subscribers. He had learned that sometimes the best way to push through one's plan was to stay in the background. "I ever after practis'd it on such occasions," he wrote, "and, from my frequent successes, can heartily recommend it. The present little sacrifice of your vanity will afterwards be amply repaid." Franklin was repaid with a chance to read the books, hopefully at least two hours a day, to make up for the formal schooling he never had.

The Library Company of Philadelphia soon grew to more than 100 members. It remains a Philadelphia institution today with more than 500,000 volumes.

Franklin's next project was less intellectual but more practical. He had observed that Philadelphia, unlike Boston, lacked an organized method of fighting fires. At the time most buildings were made of wood, and a fire that ran out of control could level a city. There was no lack of bravery and willingness, he wrote in the *Pennsylvania Gazette*, but there was little organization.

THE FIRE COMPANY

In 1733 Franklin proposed the formation of a volunteer fire company. With his usual attention to detail, quoted by Lemay, he described how operations would be directed by wardens carrying "a red staff of five feet long." Under their command would be men who carried specific equipment and had specific duties. Some would carry axes or hooks, and others would operate pumping engines or wield leather buckets filled with water.

In 1735 he incorporated his plan in a letter supposedly written to the *Gazette* by an "old citizen" who proclaimed, quoted by Brands, "An ounce of prevention is worth a pound of cure." He listed some precautions homeowners could take, but then said that "a Club or Society of active Men," should be formed "whose business is to tend all fires . . . wherever they happen."

Reaction among Philadelphians to the letter was encouraging, so in 1736 Franklin and 19 neighbors organized the Union Fire Company. The number of members was set at 25 and later raised to 30. More wanted to join, but Franklin instead encouraged separate companies to be set up in other parts of the city, much as he had suggested the idea of the Junto be spread.

Franklin was an active member of the company, missing only two of the monthly meetings from 1737 to 1738. As he developed other interests, he began to skip meetings, paying the one shilling fine, but he still fought fires. Early in 1743 an announcement, quoted by Lemay, appeared in the *Gazette* offering a reward for the return of a leather bucket "marked B. FRANKLIN & Co." Decades later, after Franklin returned from France following the American Revolution, he would meet with the four remaining original company members, each man bringing his leather bucket.

THE POLICE FORCE

Even before his fire protection project was completed, Franklin turned to the issue of crime prevention. Philadelphia, as with most colonial towns, had no organized police force, leaving law enforcement to constables hired separately by each ward, or section, of the city. Citizens were supposed to take turns helping the constables keep watch at night, but most paid a small fine to be excused. Instead of using these fines to hire assistants, however, the constables, according to his *Autobiography*, "often got such ragamuffins about him as a watch, that respectable housekeepers did not choose to mix with" and spent most of their watch time drinking.

In 1735 Franklin outlined the problem in a paper for the Junto. Not only did he propose, as quoted by Lemay, that "proper men" be hired, but also that they should be paid through "a Tax that should be proportion'd to Property." Why, he argued, should a poor widow and a wealthy merchant pay the same amount? The tax, rather, should be one "respecting the Circumstances of those who paid it." He thus became one of the earliest advocates of progressive taxation.

His plan, however, would have to wait. Unlike the fire company, taxation for a police force was a governmental issue and would require action by the Pennsylvania Assembly. In 1743 the city asked for such action but did not get it. A similar request two years later was likewise ignored by the assembly.

It was not until after Franklin was elected to the Philadelphia Common Council in 1748 that another request, according to his *Autobiography*, "paved the Way for the Law . . . when the Members of our Clubs were grown into more Influence." The law was passed in January 1751. That summer Franklin, by then a member of the assembly, drafted the regulations.

The plan actually improved on Franklin's initial proposal in that it included street lighting in addition to a constabulary, but Franklin was able to improve on it further, combining public service with his inventiveness. He found that the globe lamps brought from London did not admit enough air and thus tended to fill with smoke. They could also easily be broken. He came up with a new design of four flat panes surmounted by a metal cap. These, according to his *Autobiography*, "continu'd bright till morning, and an accidental stroke would generally break but a single pane, easily repair'd."

"POLLY BAKER"

For a man living in the eighteenth century, Franklin had a remarkably modern view of the role of women. He held a dim view, for instance, of the way that different moral and legal standards were applied to women as compared to men. His most pointed condemnation of such discrimination came in a 1747 article, "The Speech of Polly Baker," written anonymously by Franklin pretending to be a woman who had been fined by a Connecticut court for having a fifth child out of wedlock.

In her speech, which was printed in *The Maryland Gazette* on April 15, 1747, and can now be found on the TeachingAmericanHistory.org Web site, the fictitious woman said:

"I cannot conceive . . . what the Nature of my Offence is. . . . Can it be a Crime . . . to add to the Number of the King's Subjects, in a new Country that really wants People? . . . You believe I have offended Heaven, and must suffer eternal Fire: Will not that be sufficient? . . . But how can it be believed,

THE PHILOSOPHICAL SOCIETY

The American Philosophical Society was another idea that did not originate with Franklin, but that he turned into reality. In 1739 John Bartram, a Philadelphia farmer and botanist, suggested the creation of an academy, somewhat like Britain's Royal Society. His proposal lagged until 1743 when Franklin promoted it in a widely distributed pamphlet. He pointed out that there were no doubt men throughout the colonies who, from time to time, had ideas that "might produce discoveries to the advantage of some or all of the British Plantations [colonies], or to the Benefit of Mankind in general."

that Heaven is angry at my having Children, when. . . God has been pleased to add his divine Skill and admirable Workmanship in the Formation of their Bodies, and crown'd it by furnishing them with rational and immortal Souls?. . . And on the other hand, take into your wise Consideration, the great and growing Number of Batchelors in the Country, many of whom. . . by their Manner of Living, leave unproduced. . . Hundreds of their Posterity . . . Is not theirs a greater Offence against the Public Good, than mine?. . . I have hazarded the Loss of the public Esteem, and frequently incurr'd public Disgrace and Punishment; and therefore ought, in my humble Opinion, instead of a Whipping, to have a Statue erected to my Memory."

The story was widely printed in both America and Europe. Thirty years later Franklin told the truth about Polly Baker, explaining that he'd made up the tale to amuse readers on a slow news day.

THE
AMERICAN PHILOSOPHICAL SOCIET'
~ *FOUNDED BY* ~
BENJAMIN FRANKLIN
- 1 7 4 3 -

Outgrowth of The Junto, 1727 : Reorganized, 1769
THE FIRST LEARNED SOCIETY IN
THE BRITISH PLANTATIONS IN AMERICA

This Building was Erected 1786-1789

Franklin created the American Philosophical Society because he felt that, once the hard labor of establishing the colonies was complete, there was time for scholarly and artistic pursuits in America. Many founders of the republic were members, including George Washington, John Adams, Thomas Jefferson, Alexander Hamilton, and James Madison.

With his usual thoroughness, he went on to describe exactly how such persons would share their ideas, which specific branches of the sciences the society would address, and why it should be located in Philadelphia.

The society began meeting formally in 1744. In keeping with Franklin's lifelong viewpoint, members concentrated on projects that would benefit ordinary people, such as map improvement, livestock breeding, crops, and even how to brew a better beer.

Despite Franklin's best efforts, nothing much was accomplished and he grumbled, as quoted by Lemay, that the members "are very idle Gentleman; they will take no pains." Twenty years later, however, the American Philosophical Society was revived and went on to prosper, taking part in such events as the Lewis and Clark exploration of the American West and the expedition during which the Antarctic continent was discovered. It continues to attract some of the most outstanding scientific minds in the United States and from abroad. The society library includes many of Franklin's personal volumes.

THE ACADEMY

Franklin's next civic project had equally important and long-lasting effects on learning. He had first proposed the idea of establishing a university a year earlier, but nothing came of it. Never one to let go of a good idea, however, he revived it in 1749 in a pamphlet. It was not right, he wrote, that Pennsylvania lacked an "academy" to go alongside the already established Harvard, William and Mary, Princeton, and Yale.

Franklin's university, however, would be different. Primarily, unlike the other four, it would not be affiliated with any religious denomination. Emphasis would be on practical subjects such as business, writing, accounting, and speech. Franklin still regarded Harvard as elitist and wrote that Pennsylvania Academy students would live "plainly, temperately, and frugally." His proposal included much detail, even more than was usual for Franklin. He not only listed what subjects should be taught, but how they should be taught, including details of pronunciation.

The purpose of the pamphlet was to help raise money, and Franklin quickly raised £2,000 (about $320,000). Classes were to be held in the Great Hall, a building he had been instrumental in building for evangelistic preacher George Whitefield years before, but which had been abandoned. Classes began in 1751, and the academy's name was changed in 1791 to the University of Pennsylvania.

Franklin involved himself not only in the establishment and housing of the university, but in its governance. He was a member of the first board of trustees and remained a member all his life. In his *Autobiography*, he wrote that he had "had the very great pleasure of seeing a number of the youth who have receiv'd their education in it, distinguish'd by their improv'd abilities, serviceable in public stations and ornaments to their country."

THE MILITIA PLAN

At the same time that Franklin was trying to improve police protection in Philadelphia he was also working toward protecting all of Pennsylvania. The western part of the colony was a frontier area bordering on the area controlled by the French. It was the site of numerous small wars between the British and French and their Indian allies. One such war broke out in 1744, and French ships began raids up the Delaware River, which formed Pennsylvania's eastern border.

The assembly, dominated by Quakers opposed to armed conflict, would not authorize any defensive measures, so Franklin decided to take charge. In November 1747 he anonymously wrote and published a pamphlet that warned what horrors might befall an undefended Philadelphia. He answered, since neither the assembly nor the Penn family, owners of the colony, seemed willing to defend the people, who would do so. "We, the middling people," he wrote, as quoted by Isaacson. "The tradesmen, shopkeepers and farmers of this province city!"

This had what Franklin called in his *Autobiography* "a sudden and surprising effect." He followed it with a long article in the *Gazette* describing exactly how a militia would be organized. Somewhat against his customary practice, he made two public speeches. Soon, almost 10,000 men had joined and formed themselves into local companies. Franklin was elected colonel by his Philadelphia company, but he refused the rank and instead served as an ordinary soldier.

The formation of the militia put Franklin squarely at odds with the Penn family. Writing the association's charter, he used wording, as quoted by Isaacson, that seemed to anticipate the Declaration of Independence: "Being thus unprotected by the government . . . we do hereby, for our mutual defense and security . . . form ourselves into an Association." It was no wonder that Thomas Penn wrote, as quoted by Isaacson, that the militia was "little less than treason" and that Franklin "is a dangerous man."

THE HOSPITAL

It would seem to be natural, given Franklin's belief in doing good for his neighbors, for him to be involved in health care. But he did so only after a good friend, Dr. Thomas Bond, came up with the idea. Bond had studied in Europe and had observed hospitals there. When Bond began talking to people about establishing a hospital in Philadelphia, everyone asked him what Franklin thought of the idea.

Bond had not yet asked Franklin, but when he did he received an enthusiastic reception. Franklin quickly prepared a petition, had it signed by more than 30 leading citizens, and presented it to the assembly. There was some resistance. Rural delegates objected to the expense, thinking the hospital would benefit city dwellers only.

Franklin then hit on a novel way to change their minds. He said he would raise £2,000 if the assembly would agree to raise an equal sum. The assembly agreed, thinking he would never raise the money. Franklin raised more than enough, the assembly kept its promise, and Philadelphia Hospital opened in 1752. This idea for raising funds, a so-called matching grant, is now widespread.

Franklin took pride in the creation of the hospital and, in his *Autobiography*, confessed to being pleased with his own political maneuvering. He considered the project so important, he wrote, that he "more easily excus'd myself for having made some use of cunning."

That cunning would soon be put to many other uses. His various civic projects had put Franklin in close contact with the political leaders of his day, and it was little wonder that, now retired from the printing business, he took up the business of government.

5

The Road to Revolution

Benjamin Franklin was not a revolutionary by nature. He was a loyal subject of Great Britain. His vision for the colonies was a place within the British Empire. Only gradually, through a long battle with the colony's owners over its citizens' rights, did he come to understand that Britain did not share his vision.

Franklin was no stranger to politics, having been a member of the Philadelphia Common Council since 1748. He also had been clerk of the Pennsylvania Assembly since 1736 and had brought some of his ideas for civic improvement to that body. He must have felt, however, that he would be able to accomplish much more if he were a member rather than an employee or a petitioner.

Even so, he twice turned down a chance to run for a seat as one of Philadelphia's representatives to the assembly. In 1751, however, a special election was held to fill a vacancy, and Franklin was elected. "I conceived becoming a member would enlarge my powers of doing good," he wrote in his *Autobiography*, but then admitted, "I would not, however, insinuate that my ambition was not flatter'd."

The big issue facing the assembly was one of defense. One war between Britain and France had ended in 1748, but another, one that would be known in America as the French and Indian War, was about to begin. The French were determined to limit British expansion westward and in 1753 began building a line of forts along the Ohio River with the intention of eventually linking up with their possessions in Louisiana.

Alarmed, the British government overcame its caution concerning cooperation among the colonies and asked each one to send delegates to a meeting in Albany, New York, in June 1754. One of the primary goals was to seek some method of a unified defense. Franklin was all for the idea and graphically expressed his view in the *Gazette* in one of America's most famous cartoons. It depicted a snake chopped into several sections, each bearing the name of a colony. Under the snake were the words "Join, or Die."

THE ALBANY PLAN

Not all colonies shared this view, and only seven of them sent delegates to Albany. Franklin was one of four delegates from Pennsylvania and, although the assembly had gone on record as opposing unification, had an idea for achieving just that. His "Albany Plan" called for a national congress to which colonies would send representatives based on population. There would be a chief executive appointed by the king.

The division of powers between this congress and the individual colonies was a forerunner to the United States Constitution that would come 35 years later. Congress would control defense and westward expansion, and the colonies would keep control of internal

Franklin created this cartoon, "Join, or Die," to express his feeling that the colonies should present a united defense. The cartoon has been used throughout U.S. history for various purposes by many different individuals and groups.

governance. Franklin thus introduced to America the concept that came to be known as federalism.

On July 10 the delegates approved the plan by a large margin and sent it to the individual colonial governments and to Parliament in London for approval. Franklin worked hard to secure approval in Pennsylvania. Some suggested that the king instead of colonists should choose the delegates to a congress. Franklin replied, as quoted in Carl Van Doren's *Benjamin Franklin*, "It is supposed an undoubted right of Englishmen not to be taxed but by their own consent given through their representatives." This concept of no taxation without representation would be one of the issues at the heart of the American Revolution.

Despite Franklin's efforts, Pennsylvania rejected the Albany Plan, as did every other colony and the British Parliament. After the Revolution, Franklin would reflect that this failure might have indirectly caused the Revolution. Had the colonies joined for common defense, he argued, it would not have been necessary for Britain to send troops to America and to levy taxes to pay for them and, as quoted by Isaacson, "the bloody contest it occasioned would have been avoided."

CATY RAY

When the Albany conference was over, Franklin did not return home, but instead made a leisurely tour of New England postal facilities. In 1753 he had been named one of two deputy postmasters for the colonies by the British government, and he now had a chance to see how the service was being run and to make some changes. True to form, he came up with several innovations, including America's first home delivery service.

His tour was more noteworthy to history, however, because of his acquaintance with Catherine "Caty" Ray of Boston, who was the sister-in-law of one of Franklin's relatives. Twenty-five years younger than Franklin, she was knowledgeable, a good conversationalist, and as charmed by Franklin as he was by her.

Franklin's relationship with Caty Ray was the first of many he would have with other women. There is no indication that he meant to deceive his wife. Indeed, he wrote to Caty that she need not fear anyone else reading her letters. His mildly mischievous flirtation with Caty, writes Isaacson, was typical of those that would follow, "slightly naughty in a playful way, flattering to both parties, filled with intimations of intimacy." Isaacson adds, however, that there is no evidence that Franklin had any sexual affair during his marriage.

GENERAL BRADDOCK

Meanwhile, the French and Indian War had begun. Britain sent two regiments under General Edward Braddock. His goal was to push the

French from the Ohio Valley by capturing Fort Duquesne, on the site of present-day Pittsburgh, from the French and then march north to take Fort Niagara in far western New York. When Braddock came ashore in Virginia, none of the wagons and supplies he had requested were there to meet him. The Pennsylvania Assembly had been asked to provide supplies but could not agree to do so, to Franklin's disgust, because of the Penns' objections to a tax on their lands.

Braddock was furious and threatened to march his troops back onto their ships and head for home. Franklin, part of a Pennsylvania delegation sent to greet him, told the general that his colony would provide the supplies. Once back in Philadelphia, Franklin printed pamphlets urging local farmers to provide supplies, horses, and wagons. They would be paid by the British, he said, adding that, if they did not agree, as quoted by Lemay, "violent Measures probably will be used." When the farmers remained unconvinced, Franklin pledged to cover the cost himself should the British fail to pay. Within two weeks he had rounded up 259 horses and 150 wagons.

Franklin also advised Braddock to be cautious of Indian ambushes. Braddock had no experience fighting a guerilla war, but he had plenty of confidence. According to Franklin's *Autobiography*, Braddock answered, "These savages may, indeed, be a formidable enemy to your raw American militia, but upon the king's regular and disciplin'd troops, sir, it is impossible they should make any impression." Franklin did not reply, but it came as no surprise to him when, a few weeks later, the British troops were routed by a combined force of French and Indian fighters and Braddock was killed. There were few survivors, but among them was a colonial colonel named George Washington.

The Pennsylvania Assembly, thrown into a panic by the defeat, quickly voted a sum of £50,000 for defense, but it was rejected by Governor Robert Morris, again over the issue of the taxation of Penn

British general Edward Braddock was defeated en route to Fort Duquesne in the French and Indian War. Had he heeded Franklin's warning about the Indians' guerilla tactics, he might have been spared.

family land. Franklin was enraged, especially when he found out that Morris had been ordered, as a condition of his appointment, to veto all taxes on the proprietors' lands. Franklin would hereafter be an enemy to the Penns.

THE NEW MILITIA

A compromise was reached, and Franklin took charge of organizing the new militia. He spent seven weeks in 1756 on the western frontier, overseeing the building of temporary forts. He then returned to Phila-delphia, where he was elected colonel of the city's regiment. Governor Morris reluctantly approved the election and wrote Thomas Penn, as quoted by Lemay, that Franklin and the assembly "were using every means in their Power . . . to wrest [seize] the Government out of your hands." The Penns were further angered when Franklin had the regi-ment parade past his house in a grand troop review.

It might seem odd then, given this relationship, that the assembly in 1757 voted to send Franklin to London to negotiate with the Penn family and, if unsuccessful, to plead its case to the British government. He was, however, recognized as the most able man in the assembly and had the added advantage of being wealthy enough to pay his own way. Accordingly, he sailed in June, accompanied by his son William, then about 26, but not his wife, who had a strong fear of sea travel. Franklin thought he would be gone a few months. In fact, he would be in England most of the next 15 years.

LONDON AGAIN

In London, Franklin was greeted by Peter Collinson, the library's agent, and soon found living quarters in the heart of the city. His landlady, a widow named Margaret Stevenson, and her daughter Polly, 18, served as almost a second family to their American lodger.

COLONEL FRANKLIN ON PARADE

When Franklin was able to guide a militia bill through the Pennsylvania Assembly in 1755, he knew that it was against the wishes of the Penn family, proprietors of the colony, and Governor Robert Morris. That did not stop him, however, from donning a military uniform and taking command.

The next year, however, he tried to avoid bringing attention to himself when returning to Philadelphia from a trip west to organize defenses. Learning that a large crowd was planning to ride out to meet him and escort him back to the city, as quoted in H.W. Brands's *The First American,* he "made a forced march, and got to town in the night, by which they [the citizens] were disappointed, and some a little chagrined."

Later, however, when he was elected colonel of Philadelphia's militia regiment, Franklin yielded to vanity by scheduling a grand review of his troops. Company after company marched past a reviewing stand, paused, fired a volley into the air, and marched on. Then came four cannon, gaudily painted, followed by musicians playing fifes and drums. Last of all came Franklin, riding a horse. The *Pennsylvania Gazette* reported, as quoted in Walter Isaacson's *Benjamin Franklin,* that "so grand an appearance was never before seen in Pennsylvania."

The Penns and Governor Morris were likely even more displeased a few days later when, on his departure for a trip to Virginia, Franklin was escorted out of the city by a troop of soldiers, their swords drawn. Franklin, who had not known what was planned, wrote, as quoted by Isaacson, that "this silly affair greatly increased his [Thomas Penn's] rancor against me."

Stevenson accompanied Franklin on numerous social occasions, and he treated Polly like a daughter. Indeed, he seemed more affectionate in his subsequent letters to the Stevensons than he did to his family in Philadelphia. As with Catherine Ray, however, there was no indication of anything more than friendship and a mild flirtation.

There was nothing friendly about Franklin's meetings with Thomas and Richard Penn. Franklin presented the assembly's requests that the governor be allowed to use his own judgment in matters involving taxation. As quoted by Isaacson, the document called exempting the Penns' property from taxes "unjust and cruel." The Penns promptly turned the matter over to their lawyers, who delayed a ruling for almost a year.

In the meantime, Franklin's meetings with Thomas Penn went from bad to worse. The culmination came in January 1758 when Franklin claimed that the colony's original charter, given by Thomas's father, William, gave the assembly the same rights as Parliament had in England. Penn replied that the charter could be interpreted almost any way he wished.

Franklin was furious and wrote to Isaac Norris, speaker of the assembly, as quoted by Van Doren, that Penn had spoken "with a kind of triumphing, laughing insolence, such as a low jockey might do when a purchaser complained that he had cheated him in a horse." When this insult was reported to Penn, he grew equally angry and decreed that from then on Franklin would deal only with the family's lawyer, Ferdinand Paris.

MEETING WITH GRANVILLE

Franklin did not fare much better in his discussions with British government leaders. Shortly after his arrival, he met with Lord Granville, a member of the king's inner circle. Franklin said that colonists should have the same rights as Englishmen and their elected assemblies the same rights as Parliament. To his surprise and disappointment, Granville immediately disagreed. He later recalled Granville as having said, as quoted by Isaacson, "You

Americans have wrong ideas of the nature of your constitution." He went on to say that the king's word, as relayed by colonial governors, was the law and must be obeyed. This was Franklin's first inkling that the British government considered Americans second-class citizens.

The Penns did not reply to Franklin's petition on behalf of the assembly until November 1758, but Franklin was far from idle while he waited. His experiments with electricity had made him famous throughout Britain. He had been elected a member of the Royal Society while still in America and now had a chance to attend meetings and exchange information with the greatest scientists of the day. He was equally at home with writers and journalists and was a frequent and popular visitor at the coffeehouses they patronized.

When Franklin finally got his answer from the Penns, through Ferdinand Paris, they said that their instructions to governors were the law and could not be changed by the assembly. They mentioned the possibility of taxation, but in vague language that could be interpreted almost any way.

ANOTHER STRATEGY

Franklin could have gone home, but he did not. He was reluctant to give up his mission as a failure, and he might well have grown so fond of the stimulating life in London that he wished to stay there. Since the Penns considered the matter closed and would not deal with him, he chose another strategy, trying to convince the British government to make Pennsylvania a Crown colony, subject to the king instead of the Penns. There was no logical reason to think the government would agree. Gordon Wood, in his biography *The Americanization of Benjamin Franklin*, called Franklin's tactic "political blindness," adding that his anger toward the Penns had clouded his judgment.

Sure enough, Franklin's proposal made no headway, but he did achieve one success. In 1759 Lord Mansfield, another member of the king's council, offered a compromise on taxation. The Penns' undeveloped and unsurveyed land would be taxed the same as other similar property.

Franklin continued to press his case and to remain in England. He and William spent the summer of 1759 in Scotland, where he visited with such personages as economist Adam Smith, church leader Alexander Carlyle, and philosopher/historian David Hume. He visited St. Andrews University, where he was given an honorary doctorate and was always thereafter referred to, both in Europe and America, as "Doctor Franklin." Three years later he received a similar honor from Oxford University.

In early 1760 Franklin was still not ready to rejoin his family in Philadelphia, but instead made an effort to have his family join him in London. His idea was for Deborah and Sally to come to England and for Sally to marry William Strahan, son of a London friend. Deborah once more refused to leave Philadelphia.

WILLIAM'S APPOINTMENT

Franklin's son, William, however, did have marital plans. His father had wanted him to marry Polly Stevenson, but William had his eye on Elizabeth Downes, a woman with higher social connections. Franklin did not entirely approve. He was afraid that William was more interested in achieving high status than following his father's preference for being a tradesman. That fear increased when William, apparently with no help from Franklin, secured a royal appointment as the governor of New Jersey.

William did, however, follow in Franklin's footsteps in another way. In 1760 he acknowledged he was the father of an illegitimate child, Temple Franklin, but nothing about the mother is known. The boy was put with foster parents when William returned to America, but in later years he would have a warm and close relationship with his grandfather.

Franklin's relationship with William, however, had grown cool, although they traveled to the Netherlands together in 1761. But the next year, when Franklin finally decided to return to America, he elected to sail on August 24 and thus attended neither William's wedding two weeks later nor his formal installation as a royal governor by the new king, George III.

Once back in Philadelphia, Franklin stayed only a few months. In April 1763 he took off on a seven-month tour of postal facilities, taking his daughter, Sally, with him. When he returned, Pennsylvania had a new governor, John Penn, nephew of Thomas Penn. Franklin was hopeful at first that Penn would prove more reasonable than his predecessors. But this was not the case. Penn and the assembly clashed over numerous issues, including taxation The governor vetoed a bill that the assembly had drafted according to the compromise worked out in London.

Not everyone in the assembly was on Franklin's side. His enemies, who were allies of the Penns and others opposed to his Crown colony idea, conspired to defeat him for re-election in October 1764. His supporters, however, still had control of the assembly, which voted to send him to England once more to present a petition against the Penns.

And so, after only 29 months back home, Franklin sailed for London. As before, he wrote to Deborah that his duties should occupy only a few months. As before, he was wrong. More than 10 years would pass before he returned, and when he returned it would be as a rebel.

6

Rebel

When Benjamin Franklin left on his second diplomatic mission to England in 1765, he still had hopes
that the government would change its policies toward
the American colonies and keep them part of the
British Empire. Over the years those hopes faded and
then disappeared altogether. When Franklin returned,
the first shots of the American Revolution had been
fired and the Declaration of Independence was on the
horizon.

Back in London, Franklin quickly reestablished
his substitute family, moving into his old rooms at
Mrs. Stevenson's house. Polly was still there and took
on the role of big sister when Franklin brought his
grandson, Temple, now four years old, to live with
them. He did not acknowledge the relationship,

even to the Stevensons, until after his return to America years later.

The relationship between Britain and America, however, was about to get worse. Parliament passed the Stamp Act, which would require that every legal document, book, newspaper, and deck of cards bear a stamp showing that a tax had been paid. The act was necessary, the government said, to pay the cost of the French and Indian War.

Franklin argued against passage of the Stamp Act, but his protests were relatively mild. He adopted the attitude that Parliament was so much in favor of the tax that stronger statements against it would not only be useless, but would also hurt America's cause. In a letter, quoted in Isaacson, Franklin wrote, "We might well have hindered the sun's setting."

This attitude was one of the worst political blunders of Franklin's career. The people of Philadelphia were furious at Parliament for levying the tax and furious at Franklin for not doing more to prevent it. Indeed, one friend wrote to him, as quoted by Isaacson, that the people had "imbibed the notion that you had a hand in framing it." Their anger was so strong that a mob marched on his house, intending to burn it to the ground. Deborah had sent Sally to safety in New Jersey but had stayed to protect her home as best she could. Fortunately an armed band of Franklin's supporters intervened, and the mob dispersed.

Anger at the Stamp Act was widespread throughout the colonies and energized such new leaders as Patrick Henry, Thomas Jefferson, and Samuel Adams. Still, Franklin urged moderation. It was not until the end of 1765 and after many more letters from home that he set out to repair his reputation, writing a series of essays attacking the Stamp Act. In one, as quoted by Isaacson, he warned that the tax was "creating a deep-rooted aversion between the two countries and laying the foundation of a future total separation." He argued the colonies' case before Parliament early in 1766, with a new party in power, and the Stamp Act was repealed.

THE TOWNSHEND ACTS

Soon after the repeal of the Stamp Act, another took its place. In June 1767 the Townshend Acts, named for Britain's chief financial officer, imposed a tax on several items, including tea. Once more, Franklin was out of step with his colonial countrymen. While protestors led by Samuel Adams demonstrated in Boston, Franklin urged caution and patience. For more than a year he walked a fine line, trying to appease the Americans as well as the British government. In August 1768, however, after a bitter argument with Lord Hillsborough, secretary of state for the colonies, he came down on the side of the Americans and began to attack the Townshend Acts, which he wrote, as quoted by Isaacson, might "convert millions of the King's loyal subjects into rebels."

Parliament, too, had misjudged the furor the Townshend Acts caused in America and was looking for a compromise. On March 5, 1770, it began debating a partial repeal. Ironically, on the same day, British soldiers fired on a group of protestors, killing five in what became known as the Boston Massacre. A few weeks later, all the taxes were lifted, except for that on tea.

In the meantime, Franklin had been dealing with both his real and substitute families. In 1767 Sally fell in love with Richard Bache, owner of a struggling Philadelphia store. Deborah wrote, as quoted by Isaacson, that she had been "obliged to be father and mother." If she suspected this would bring Franklin home, she was wrong. Instead of returning to deal with the matter, Franklin went to France for an extended vacation, leaving the decision in Deborah's hands. He came back to London to find that the wedding had already taken place.

Nothing, it seemed, could induce Franklin to return to America, not Sally's wedding, not a stroke suffered by Deborah early in

1769, and not the birth of Sally's son Benjamin, with whom he would later form a relation as close as that with his other grandson, Temple. There was one occasion, however, that he would not miss, the wedding of Polly Stevenson. She had delayed more than a year, seeking Franklin's approval. He finally relented and walked her down the aisle in the summer of 1770.

By this time, Franklin was losing hope that Britain and its American colonies could reach a compromise. In one report, quoted by James Srodes in *Franklin: The Essential Founding Father*, he wrote that he feared a "bloody struggle [that will] end in absolute slavery to America, or ruin to Britain by the loss of her colonies."

THE AUTOBIOGRAPHY

His diplomatic mission, for all practical purposes, was ended, but still Franklin remained in Europe. In 1771 he spent months touring England, including a visit to a friend's house at Twyford, just outside Winchester. It was there, in July 1771, that he began his autobiography. While it took the form of a letter to his son William, it was meant to be eventually published. He wrote the first eight chapters at Twyford, then put the work aside, not resuming writing until 1788.

It would not be until late 1772 that Franklin would immerse himself once more, inadvertently, in politics. A member of Parliament who was friendly to America slipped Franklin copies of letters written by Thomas Hutchinson, the royal governor of Massachusetts, recommending methods of dealing with the colonists. One of them, as quoted by Srodes advised that "there must be an abridgement of what are called English liberties."

Franklin sent the letters to his friend Thomas Cushing in Massachusetts, asking that they not be published. His goal was to show Cushing and others that it was royal governors, not the British government, who were the problem and that they should continue to negotiate. Cushing, however, published the letters, which only served to push American anger to new heights.

That anger grew even more fierce in 1773 when Parliament passed the Tea Act. This act left the tax in place and increased the cost of tea in America by giving the East India Company exclusive importing rights. Franklin was worried that this might cause violence, and he was right. On the night of December 16, Samuel Adams and his Sons of Liberty, dressed as Indians, boarded a ship and tossed 342 chests of tea into Boston Harbor.

Despite his increasingly rebel leanings, Franklin was shocked at what he thought a wanton destruction of private property. He was afraid the so-called Boston Tea Party would make Britain take a

SUNDAY IN FLANDERS

In 1761 Franklin made one of his many summer trips from England to the European continent. He could not go to France because the two countries were at war, but went instead to the Netherlands and to the county of Flanders, which is now divided among the Netherlands, France, and Belgium. One aspect of life there that drew his attention was how the people spent Sundays as compared to those in America.

"In the afternoon," he wrote, as quoted by Walter Isaacson in *Benjamin Franklin: An American Life,* "both high and low went to the play or the opera, where there was plenty of singing, fiddling, and dancing. I looked for God's judgments, but saw no sign of them."

He went on to observe that God evidently did not object to amusement on Sundays as much as the American Puritans believed. The cheerfulness of the people of Flanders, he wrote, "would almost make one suspect that the Deity is not so angry at that offense as a New England justice."

harsher line with America. Again, he was right, and he himself was one of the first targets.

In January 1774, Franklin was ordered to appear before the royal council. He was told that he must testify on a demand by the Massachusetts Assembly to remove Governor Hutchinson. The real reason the council wanted Franklin to appear, however, was to try to find out how the Hutchinson letters had been obtained.

IN THE COCKPIT

The hearing before the royal council was in the Cockpit in Whitehall Palace, so called because cockfights had been conducted there. The council's treatment of Franklin was equally savage. The prosecutor, Alexander Wedderburn, began by heaping abuse on Franklin for more than an hour. The audience, consisting mostly of Franklin's enemies, hooted and jeered. Franklin, however, according to a witness quoted by Isaacson, "stood conspicuously erect, without the smallest movement of any part of his body." When the time finally came for him to speak, he remained silent.

The Massachusetts demand was, of course, rejected, and Franklin learned the next day that he had been removed from his place as deputy postmaster. But even with this source of income removed and despite his public humiliation in the Cockpit, Franklin still delayed returning home. He went into hiding for a time, fearing arrest, then maintained a very low profile for several months.

Then, in December, he received a letter from William telling him that Deborah had died. Despite her letters hinting that her illness was due to stress caused by his absence, Franklin had responded only with cheerful generalities. William's letter, as quoted by Isaacson, seemed intended to produce guilt. "She told me that she never expected to see you unless you returned this winter," he wrote. "I heartily wish you had happened to come over in the fall, as I think her disappointment preyed a good deal on her spirits."

Still, Franklin delayed, spending additional weeks in unofficial talks. It was not until March 1775 that he boarded a ship for America. While he was at sea, a troop of British soldiers sent to arrest the ringleaders of the Boston radicals were routed by the "minutemen" in Concord, Massachusetts. The American Revolution had begun.

BECOMING A RADICAL

Franklin was accompanied on the trip by his grandson Temple. About a month after their return, they met with William Franklin, who had not seen his son, now 14, since birth. The result of the reunion was that Temple was to stay with his father in New Jersey, but only through the summer, after which he was to live and go to school in Philadelphia.

Temple was not the only point of contention between Franklin and his son. William Franklin was a committed Tory, an American who remained loyal to Britain, while Franklin had all but publicly declared for independence. The split was personal as well as political, and the two remained estranged.

At first, however, Franklin kept his views to himself, taking the temperature of his countrymen. He had been elected a member of the Second Continental Congress the day after his arrival but was so noncommittal that some delegates thought he might be spying on them for the British. On July 5, 1775, however, he made his sentiments known. In a letter to a friend in England, circulated in America but never actually sent to England, he wrote, as quoted by Isaacson, "You have begun to burn our towns, and murder our people. Look upon your hands! They are stained with the blood of your relations! You and I were long friends: You are now my enemy, and I am, Yours, B. Franklin."

Philad.ª July 5. 1775

Mr. Strahan,

You are a Member of Parliament, and one of that Majority which has doomed my Country to Destruction — You have begun to burn our Towns, and murder our People. — Look upon your Hands! — They are stained with the Blood of your Relations! — You and I were long Friends: — You are now my Enemy, — and

I am,

Yours,

B Franklin

Franklin wrote this letter to British Parliament member William Strahan, who had voted with Parliament to label the colonists as rebels. Franklin circulated the letter in the colonies but never actually sent it to Strahan.

Once Franklin was committed, he was fully committed. He became the most radical of the radicals. John Adams wrote, as quoted by Isaacson, that Franklin "does not hesitate at our boldest measures, but rather seems to think us too irresolute."

One of his boldest actions was, in July, to present for consideration his Article of Confederation and Perpetual Union. It was much like his previous Albany Plan but provided that the united colonies would exist outside the British Empire, unless Parliament reversed course. There would be one legislative body, but instead of a single head of state, a 12-man executive council would share responsibility. The Congress was not yet prepared to go so far, and Franklin did not insist on a vote.

PREPARING FOR WAR

But, declaration or not, America was at war. The Battle of Bunker Hill had been fought, and the city of Charleston, South Carolina, was burned by the British. Along with war came preparation for independence. A postal system was needed, and Franklin was the logical choice to head it. He donated his salary to help take care of the wounded. He was also in charge of implementing a system of currency.

Most of his duties, however, involved the military. In October he went on behalf of the Congress to Massachusetts to meet with George Washington to discuss ways to hold the militias together through the winter. Washington emphasized the need for money and supplies, a plea he would make throughout the Revolution.

By May of 1776, the people were more ready for independence than ever. Thousands were reading Thomas Paine's pamphlet *Common Sense*, which many people thought had been written by Franklin. Some troops were beginning to fly a flag, suggested by a Franklin article, showing a rattlesnake with 13 rattles and the motto "Don't Tread on Me." Congress ordered the removal of all royal governors, including William Franklin, who was arrested and held prisoner.

The stage was set for a formal declaration. On June 7 the Virginia delegation presented a resolution "to declare the United Colonies free and independent States, absolved from all allegiance to, or dependence upon, the Crown or Parliament of Great Britain." On June 11, with only the New York delegation opposed, the Congress appointed five men—Benjamin Franklin, Thomas Jefferson, John Adams, Robert R. Livingston, and Roger Sherman—to produce a document. This committee selected Jefferson to write the first draft, which he did alone.

THE DECLARATION

When he finished the draft, Jefferson first sent it to Adams and then, after making some alterations, to Franklin. In a cover note he wrote, as quoted by Isaacson, "Will Doctor Franklin be so good as to peruse it and suggest such alterations as his more enlarged view of the subject will dictate."

Most of Franklin's changes were very minor, but there was one exception. He changed Jefferson's "We hold these truths to be sacred and undeniable" to "We hold these truths [equality, life, liberty, and the pursuit of happiness] to be self-evident." The underlying premise of the Declaration thus was changed from one of religion to one of rationality, much more in keeping with Franklin's viewpoint.

There would be many more changes, some involving the elimination of entire paragraphs and sections. On July 2, the Congress voted to declare independence, but it was not until July 4 that the Declaration itself was approved.

Despite the widespread notion that the Declaration of Independence was signed on July 4, 1776, the formal signing did not take place until August 2. John Hancock, president of the Congress, was the first to sign, saying, as quoted by Van Doren, "We must be

After Thomas Jefferson drafted the Declaration of Independence, he passed it by John Adams and Benjamin Franklin. Franklin made a significant revision.

unanimous; there must be no pulling different ways; we must all hang together." Franklin's famous reply was "Yes, we must indeed all hang together, or most assuredly we shall all hang separately."

The Americans knew that their chances of defeating Britain militarily were slim without outside help. The logical place to turn for assistance was to Britain's traditional enemy, France. Accordingly, Congress chose three men to seek both recognition and a treaty: Franklin, Silas Deane of Connecticut, and Arthur Lee of Virginia. Franklin was in poor health but was determined to make the trip. He said, as quoted on the Web site of the Pennsylvania Historical and Museum Commission, "I am but a fag end [as storekeepers called the remnant from a bolt of cloth], and you may have me for what you please."

And so, on October 27, 1776, Franklin set sail for Europe once more. With him were grandsons Temple, 17, and Benjamin Bache, 7. "If I die," he later wrote, as quoted by Isaacson, "I have a child to close my eyes." Many more years and many great accomplishments come to pass, however, before that day came.

7

Diplomat

When Benjamin Franklin left the newly independent United States of America for France in 1776, the fate of the infant nation was just as much in his hands as in General George Washington's. Assistance from France was crucial to the success of the revolution, and it took all of Franklin's wisdom, wit, and cunning to bring it about.

Franklin was already famous in France for his scientific experiments, particularly those in electricity, and for *Poor Richard's Almanack.* He would become even more famous to the French, however, as a symbol of America. He was robust, hardworking, inventive, self-reliant, unspoiled by the stratified society of Europe, and fixed on the future instead of bound by the past. The notion that being closer to nature brings out the natural goodness in humans was very popular in France, largely due to the philosopher Jean-Jacques Rousseau, who was still alive when Franklin arrived.

Franklin played this idea for all it was worth. To ward off the winter chill, he wore a fur cap he had acquired on a mission to Canada. When the cap became such a sensation that fashionable ladies had their hair done to resemble it, Franklin made a point of wearing it on all sorts of occasions, even some calling for formal dress. In a society where extravagant clothes and powdered wigs were the rule, he wore plain suits and no wig. Once, when calling on King Louis XVI at the great Palace of Versailles, one witness, quoted by Isaacson, said of Franklin, "I should have taken him for a big farmer."

However rustic he wished to appear to the outside world, Franklin's private life was anything but moderate. A wealthy merchant who hoped to gain trading ties in America allowed Franklin to stay, rent free, at a large manor house at Passy, a village midway between Paris and Versailles. There were gardens in which to stroll, a legion of servants, extravagant multicourse dinners, and an extensive wine collection. Franklin's grandson Temple was Franklin's secretary while his other grandson "Benny" went to a boarding school.

THE DELEGATION

Also serving with Franklin on the American delegation were Silas Deane, with whom Franklin got along well, and Arthur Lee, with whom he did not. Deane, however, was recalled for mishandling funds, and his place was taken the following year by John Adams, who would be a constant thorn in Franklin's side.

Lee, who was responsible for Deane's removal, was also highly critical of Franklin, his rival for a land grant years before. He was also very suspicious of the delegation's secretary, Edward Bancroft, and with good reason. Bancroft worked as a British spy throughout the

Revolutionary War, sending messages written between the lines of letters in invisible ink.

The American delegation dealt with the Count de Vergennes, the French foreign minister. Their first meeting was on December 28, 1776, and Franklin at once proposed an alliance. Vergennes was open to any scheme that might hurt Britain but was not ready to commit. France's economy was in poor shape and a war with Britain would be expensive, so the French stalled, waiting to see which way the war went.

While the French waited, Franklin embarked on what amounted to a public relations campaign. He had documents on the American cause translated and published. He wrote anonymous essays for newspapers. He sought appointments with various public officials and members of the nobility to plead his case.

PHILADELPHIA CAPTURED

That case suffered a setback in September 1777 when British troops, under General William Howe, captured Philadelphia. It was a personal as well as diplomatic misfortune for Franklin. His house was confiscated, his daughter and family forced to flee, and his personal belongings stolen.

An even worse military defeat seemed imminent. General John Burgoyne was leading a force from Canada down the Hudson River Valley. If he linked up with Howe, all New England would be cut off from the other colonies. But on October 7, he was surrounded by a superior American force near Saratoga, New York, and surrendered his entire army.

The Battle of Saratoga was a turning point in the American Revolution, showing that the United States literally had a fighting chance against Britain. The significance of this victory was not lost on the French. Two days after learning of the battle, King Louis XVI signed a paper prepared by Vergennes inviting the delegates to resubmit their

On March 20, 1778, Franklin was received at the court of France. Franklin brokered an alliance with France that helped America successfully break from England.

proposal for an alliance. An agreement was quickly reached. France agreed to recognize the United States and to sign treaties for trade and a military alliance. The only catches were that France's ally, Spain, had to agree, and that France had to agree to terms of any future American treaty with Britain.

The British were alarmed by the defeat at Saratoga and by the proposed alliance, the details of which they learned from Bancroft. Faced with the threat of losing their American colonies, they sent an unofficial envoy, Paul Wentworth, to Paris to see if something could be salvaged. Franklin at first refused to see Wentworth but changed his mind when Spain unexpectedly rejected the alliance.

Wentworth's offer was that America would have its own congress with control over all internal matters. Parliament would govern only foreign relations and foreign trade. Franklin made no promises but he also made sure the French knew of Wentworth's visit.

Now it was France's turn to be alarmed. Two days after Franklin's meeting with Wentworth, Vergennes sent an official asking what it would take for the American delegation to break off any talks with Britain. Franklin replied that a speedy agreement to the original proposal would cause America to reject any agreement with Britain short of complete independence. In that case, the official said, the king would agree to an alliance regardless of Spain.

SIGNING THE TREATIES

The treaties were signed on February 6, 1778. Instead of his usual plain suit, Franklin wore one of slightly faded blue velvet. When someone asked him why, Franklin replied, as quoted by Van Doren, "To give it a little revenge. I wore this coat on the day Wedderburn abused me at Whitehall."

On March 20 King Louis XVI received the American delegation at Versailles. Amid the splendidly dressed courtiers, Franklin stood out in a plain brown suit, no wig, and no sword. His only acknowledgment of the formality of the occasion was a white hat in place of his customary fur cap.

The alliance with France did not guarantee success for the Revolution, but it is extremely doubtful if success could have been reached without it. In his *The Birth of the Republic*, Edmund Morgan calls it "the greatest diplomatic victory the United States has ever achieved."

There was much more to be done, however, and Franklin soon had a new partner with whom to do it. In April, Deane was replaced by John Adams, a man thoroughly different in temperament from Franklin. Where Franklin was witty and fun-loving, relishing in social contact, Adams was prim, prudish, and withdrawn. He respected Franklin's abilities but deplored his manner. He never made, nor tried to make, an emotional connection with the French, but neverthe-less seemed envious of Franklin's fame. He complained, as quoted by Isaacson, that Franklin had "a monopoly of reputation here and an indecency in displaying it."

Adams was disappointed that the treaty had been completed before he arrived and stayed only slightly more than a year. During that time, however, he had plenty to say about Franklin's lifestyle, which he described, as quoted by Brands, as "a scene of continual dissipation." He was especially critical of Franklin's relationships with women, writ-ing, as quoted by Van Doren, that Franklin "had neither lost his love of beauty nor his taste for it." Adams's attitude was echoed by his wife, Abigail, when a few years later Franklin took them on a visit to the home of one of his lady friends. "I own I was highly disgusted," Abigail wrote, as quoted by Brands, "and never wish for an acquaintance with any ladies of this cast."

LADIES' MAN

The woman who so aroused Abigail Adams's scorn was Madame Anne-Catherine Helvétius, a wealthy widow who lived on a farm near Passy. She was the second of the two women Franklin was most involved with during his years in France. The first was Anne-Louise Brillon de Jouy, married with two daughters and 38 years younger than Franklin.

For two years starting in the spring of 1777, Franklin and Madame Brillon were constantly in one another's company. She would play the harpsichord for him, and they would play chess until late at night. Franklin would have taken the relationship much fur-ther, but Madame Brillon would not give in. When his letters became too ardent, she replied, as quoted by Brands, "You are a man, I am a woman, and while we might think along the same lines, we must

FRANKLIN AND JOHN PAUL JONES

During the American Revolution, Franklin had little to do with purely military affairs. A notable exception was his involvement with John Paul Jones. Jones had been conducting hit-and-run raids on the coast of Scotland, but Franklin thought he could be of more benefit in an attack on England itself in combination with land forces under the command of the Marquis de Lafayette.

When Jones complained that his ship was too slow, Franklin resolved to give him command of one that had just been built for the Americans in the Netherlands. Under British pressure, however, the Dutch refused to turn over the ship. Instead, Jones was given an older, run-down French ship, which he promptly renamed, in Franklin's honor, the *Bonhomme Richard,* as Poor Richard was known in France.

Jones and Lafayette, however, were both proud officers and did not get along. When the land assault part of the expedition was eliminated, Franklin and the French sent Jones on a mission to harass British shipping. On August 14, 1779, the *Bonhomme Richard* engaged the British warship *Serapis.* At the height of the battle, the British captain called on Jones to surrender, whereupon he called back, "I have not yet begun to fight." He rammed the *Serapis* and eventually captured it. The *Bonhomme Richard,* however, had suffered too much damage and sank.

speak and act differently. Perhaps there is no great harm in a man having desires and yielding to them; a woman may have desires, but she must not yield."

Instead, they formed a bond more like father and daughter than lovers. When they were together, she would call him "Dear Papa" and sit on his lap, much to John Adams's disapproval. Much has been made of Franklin's playing chess with her as she reclined in her bath-tub, but it was not as scandalous as it seemed since most of the tub was covered by a wooden lid.

But while Franklin might have treated Madame Brillon with fatherly affection, he failed to demonstrate such feelings for his real daughter back in Philadelphia. His letters to her, full of admonitions to live simply, seem hypocritical considering his own lifestyle. When she asked him to send her items for a ball gown, he answered, as quoted by Isaacson, "Your sending for long black pins, and lace, and feathers! disgusted me as much as if you had put salt in my strawberries."

Franklin's relationship with Madame Helvétius was much more serious. At 60, she was much closer in age to him than Madame Brillon, and she was widowed. In addition to being beautiful, she had a lively mind and an irreverent wit that matched Franklin's. He was so attracted to her that, in 1779, he proposed marriage in a half-joking way. He wrote of an upcoming meeting, as quoted by Brands, "He [Franklin] will be there early to watch her enter, with that grace and dignity which have charmed him. He even plans to capture her there and keep her to himself for life."

While this passage might be taken as hinting at a love affair, Madame Helvétius took it and others like it as a proposal of marriage. The French finance minister, who had introduced her to Franklin, advised her to turn him down. She did so, citing the memory of her late husband. Franklin put his disappointment in a story in which he meets that husband in heaven and tells him, as quoted by Van Doren, "I have loved her, to madness; but she was cruel to me and absolutely rejected me for love of you."

DIPLOMATIC WORK

Meanwhile, there was still diplomatic work to be done. The members of the American delegation were so at odds with one another that about all they could agree on was that only one of them should be in charge. The French made it clear that the leader should be Franklin, and the American Congress agreed, giving him sole authority. Lee reluctantly agreed, and Adams returned to Massachusetts.

Adams was home only a few months, however, before he was sent back to Paris in February 1780 with instructions to negotiate a peace with Britain when the time was right. Vergennes and Franklin were both upset by this, but Congress feared that any treaty with Britain negotiated by Franklin would be too generous to France. But the French flatly refused to work with anyone except Franklin, and Adams left for the Netherlands to try to get a loan from the Dutch.

The United States was, indeed, desperately short of money, and Franklin boldly asked France for a loan, the equivalent of $130 million in today's U.S. dollars. The French could not afford such a sum but did come up with a lesser amount, enough to keep the young republic afloat.

With the loan secured, Franklin felt his work was done and wrote to Congress asking to be replaced. Instead, he was named to a commission, along with Adams and John Jay, for any future negotiations with the British. A fourth appointee, Henry Laurens, was captured on the voyage to Europe by the British and imprisoned. The fifth, Thomas Jefferson, declined.

YORKTOWN

There was, as yet, no pressing reason for the British to negotiate. That changed dramatically on October 17, 1781, when Lord Cornwallis, trapped by American and French forces at Yorktown, Virginia, surrendered his army of 8,000 men. Lord Rockingham replaced Lord North as British prime minister in March of 1782, and talks began.

Franklin was the only one of the four commissioners in Paris at the time and wound up negotiating with two separate British envoys.

The Treaty of Paris was signed by Franklin, Adams, Jay, Laurens, and Jefferson on April 3, 1783. Franklin's diplomatic work in France had been a great success.

Lord Shelburne, the colonial secretary, sent Richard Oswald as his envoy while Shelburne's rival, Foreign Secretary Charles Fox, dispatched Thomas Grenville.

Franklin met first with Oswald, who tried to convince him not to involve the French in negotiations. Franklin refused, citing the treaty provision. Later, however, after suggesting that Britain relinquish Canada as part of an agreement, Franklin did not report the proposal to Vergennes, whom he knew would oppose it since having Britain out of North America would lessen American dependence on France. Despite the concern of Adams and Congress, Franklin seemed to be open to reaching a treaty independent of the French.

Grenville arrived in May and quickly annoyed the French by suggesting that, if Britain granted independence to America, France should return some of the Caribbean islands it had won from Britain in prior wars. Vergennes replied that America was not "asking" for independence, and Franklin said, as quoted by Van Doren, "To be sure, we do not consider ourselves as under any necessity of bargaining for such a thing which is our own."

Furthermore, Grenville had been authorized to deal only with France, since Britain did not recognize the United States. Vergennes refused, telling Franklin that the Americans could negotiate for themselves. Franklin took this as permission to conduct separate negotiations with Britain, leaving France out of the picture.

FRANKLIN'S PEACE PROVISIONS

The picture cleared considerably in July when Rockingham died, Shelburne became prime minister, and Grenville was recalled. Franklin promptly drafted a proposal for peace, which he sent informally through Oswald to Shelburne. He did not send it to Vergennes. The proposal contained four provisions labeled "necessary": full independence, removal of all British troops, a recognition of boundaries, and fishing rights off the coast of Canada. There were also four "advisable" provisions: payment for destruction of property in the United States, the ceding of Canada, acknowledgment of past wrongs against the colonies, and a trading agreement. Shelburne replied that the necessary provisions seemed acceptable, but that the advisable ones should be eliminated.

In August, Jay, who had been in Paris since June but had been ill, took over negotiations when Franklin was bedridden with gout and kidney stones. Jay insisted that Oswald have clear instructions that he was to negotiate with the Americans as representatives of an independent nation. Vergennes was troubled, fearing he would be left out, but Jay insisted. In September, Oswald had a formal commission, as quoted by Isaacson, "to treat with the commissioners appointed by the colonies under the title of 13 united states."

In October, Adams finally arrived and the three commissioners began day-and-night negotiations. Franklin's four primary provisions were agreed to and a fifth was added: freedom of navigation on the Mississippi River, which was to be the United States' western boundary. On the morning of November 30, 1782, the two delegations met in Oswald's hotel suite to sign the provisional agreement that would end the Revolutionary War.

TREATY OF PARIS

The agreement was then incorporated into the Treaty of Paris, which was signed by Franklin, Adams, and Jay, along with late arrivals Laurens and Jefferson. In Benjamin West's painting depicting the signing of the treaty, the five Americans are pictured the left side, but the right side was left unfinished. The British delegation refused to pose.

Franklin's work in France now, indeed, was done, but he lingered on, making additions to his *Autobiography*, financing the first manned flight in a hydrogen balloon, inventing bifocal spectacles, and arguing—unsuccessfully—for the turkey to be the national bird instead of the bald eagle.

Jefferson was to take over Franklin's diplomatic role but said in response to a question, "No one can replace him, Sir. I am only his successor." Yet, Jefferson's skill as a diplomat was such that he was able to make peace even between Franklin and Adams.

Finally, on July 12, 1785, the time came for Franklin to say goodbye to France and the friends he had made there. Mesdames Brillon and Helvétius wrote flowery, passionate letters of farewell. Jefferson came to see him on his last day at Passy and wrote, as quoted by Isaacson, "The ladies smothered him with embraces, and on his introducing me as his successor, I told him I wished he would transfer these privileges to me, but he answered, 'You are too young a man.'"

Accompanied by Benny and Temple, Franklin sailed first to England for a frosty, businesslike meeting with his son, William, and then on to Philadelphia. He arrived on September 14, four months short of his eightieth birthday. Although he may have been looking forward to retiring, surrounded by grandchildren, to his Market Street house, his country had more tasks for him, however. And one may have been the most important of all.

8

Elder Statesman

Franklin may have wondered what kind of welcome he would receive in Philadelphia after nine years in France. Enemies such as Arthur Lee, John Adams, and the Penn family and their allies had done their best to blacken his reputation. He need not have worried. He was met at the Market Street wharf by a huge crowd, including his daughter, Sally, who threw her arms around him. Then, amid cheering, the ringing of bells, and the booming of cannons, the crowd escorted him to his front door. "The affectionate welcome I meet with from my fellow citizens," he wrote, as quoted by Van Doren, "is far beyond my expectation."

He quickly settled in, renewing friendships with the surviving members of his fire brigade and with the American Philosophical Society. He added a wing onto his house, necessary to house not only himself and the

Franklin returned to Philadelphia to a hero's welcome. This print shows Franklin arriving dockside to greetings from his daughter, Sally; her husband, Richard Bache; their son Benjamin Franklin Bache; and Judge Thomas McKean.

Bache family, but also his more than 4,000 books, which took up the addition's entire second floor. He turned his vegetable garden into a flower garden modeled on the one at Passy.

Politics, however, was never very far away. Pennsylvanians were sharply divided on what kind of government they wanted. Merchants and tradesmen—those Franklin affectionately called the "middling" class—favored a popularly elected legislature. The large landowners, those who had previously supported the Penns, were wary of too much democracy. Both sides, however, trusted Franklin and, within days of his return, asked him to run for the Executive Council. He did not need much convincing. He confessed, as quoted by Isaacson, to having "the remains of ambition from which I had imagined myself free."

He was elected overwhelmingly to the council, which then elected him as its president, the equivalent of governor. He served three terms in office, during which time important legislation was passed. The state revised its harsh penal code, doing away with the death penalty for many crimes, including burglary. The council also softened the Test Act, which called on men to swear allegiance to the state constitution before being allowed to vote or hold office.

Franklin did not take much of a day-to-day role in the council, leaving that to his vice president. Instead, he worked skillfully behind the scenes, making observations, giving advice, and working to achieve compromise. Just his mere presence and his great reputation lowered the temperature of debates.

A much greater task lay ahead, one in which Franklin would take a much more direct part. The political division in Pennsylvania was mirrored throughout the United States. There was sharp disagreement between those who favored a strong central government and those who wanted a loose confederation, with most of the power belonging to the states.

THE CONFEDERATION

The country was currently operating under the confederation model. The Articles of Confederation had been ratified in 1781, but things were not going very well. The national government had no power to tax and had to depend on grants from the states. These grants of funds were few, small, and infrequent. Consequently, Congress had no money to build a place to meet or even to pay clerks. There was no body that could speak for all states in conducting foreign policy. There was no national army, just 13 militias and 11 navies.

The weaknesses of the Articles of Confederation were most apparent in trade. The states acted like independent nations, and not very friendly nations at that. One disagreement between Virginia and Maryland led to a conference in Philadelphia in May 1787. The stated purpose was to fix some of the problems by amending the Articles of Confederation. Some delegates, such as James Madison and Alexander Hamilton, however, did not consider the Articles worth saving. What was needed, they said, was an entirely new document that would establish a strong central government. Most of the delegates agreed, but they knew that many of their countrymen did not. Therefore they did not announce their intentions but instead worked in secret.

As they gathered in the Philadelphia statehouse, the delegates were fully aware of the importance of their task, but none more so than Franklin. It was not only the future of the United States that was at stake, he thought, but also the future of democratic government. "Indeed, if it [the convention] does not do good it must do harm as it will show that we have not wisdom enough among us to govern ourselves," he wrote, as quoted by Van Doren, "and it will strengthen the opinion of some political writers that popular governments cannot long support themselves."

VARIOUS PLANS

There was no shortage of ideas at the convention, such as those brought by Virginia and by South Carolina calling for houses of Congress to be elected on the basis of population. The problem with these plans, in the eyes of states such as New Jersey, was that they clearly favored larger states. New Jersey therefore proposed a plan that would accomplish the announced purpose of the convention—to amend the Articles of Confederation.

PLEASANT DREAMS

Franklin was always on the lookout for how to make things better. He even experimented with sleep. In 1786 he wrote to the daughter of a friend, as quoted in Walter Isaacson's *Benjamin Franklin: An American Life,* a step-by-step method of ensuring pleasant dreams.

First, he wrote, eat in moderation since "less perspirable matter is produced in a given time . . . and we may sleep longer before we are made uneasy" by sweat-soaked nightclothes. His second instruction was to wear "thinner and more porous bedclothes" so the perspiration might pass through.

Finally, he wrote, if all else fails, "get up out of bed, beat up and turn your pillow, shake the bed-clothes well . . . then throw the bed open and leave it to cool; in the meantime, continuing undressed, walk about your chamber till your skin has had time to discharge its load [of perspiration], which it will do sooner as the air may be dried and cooler."

Fresh air, he wrote, was essential, but "what is necessary above all things [is] A GOOD CONSCIENCE."

Franklin was twice the average age of the delegates. Although his experience and reputation would have qualified him for the presidency of the convention, he was limited by ill health. So Franklin nominated George Washington, who was elected unanimously. As in the Pennsylvania Assembly, Franklin's presence and calm demeanor tended to restrain tempers on both sides. He presented, wrote Benjamin Rush, as quoted by Isaacson, "a spectacle of transcendent benevolence."

Personally, Franklin favored a unicameral, or single-house, Congress, elected by the people. He could see, however, that most of the delegates disagreed. The crucial issue was that of large versus small states, and both sides were becoming entrenched in their positions. This, he told the delegates, as quoted by Isaacson, was a major mistake: "Declarations of a fixed opinion, and of determined resolution never to change it, neither enlighten nor convince us. Positiveness and warmth on one side, naturally beget the like on the other."

Franklin had a compromise in mind. In a committee meeting he suggested the creation of a House of Representatives, whose members would be popularly elected in proportion to population. There would also be a Senate, with members elected by state legislatures and equal representation from each state.

On June 30 Franklin put the proposal, as modified by Roger Sherman of Connecticut, before the entire convention. "When a broad table is to be made, and the edges of planks do not fit, the artist takes a little from both and makes a good joint," he said, as quoted by Srodes. "In like manner here both sides must part with some of their demands in order that they may join in some accommodating proposition."

THE "GREAT VICTORY"

Franklin then put the compromise in the form of a motion. Another committee that included Franklin was charged with working out the details. The measure was passed on July 16. "This was Franklin's great victory in the Convention," writes Van Doren, "that he was the author of the compromise which held the delegates together at a time when they were ready to break up without forming any new Federal agreement."

The logjam was broken, but there was still much work to be done. Franklin and others argued successfully against a proposal by Hamilton that a president should be elected for life. He also helped defeat a motion that said the president should possess wealth of at least $100,000. Should that happen, he said, the presidency would be only for the rich. He said, as quoted by Isaacson, "Some of the greatest rogues I was ever acquainted with were the richest rogues."

Finally, on September 17, the new Constitution of the United States was ready for the delegates' signatures. It was not everything Franklin wanted, but he knew that it was the best they could do and far better than what had been expected. In his closing speech to the convention, as quoted by Brands, he said, "I confess that there are several parts of this constitution which I do not at present approve. But I am not sure I shall ever approve them." He went on to say, however, that "the older I grow, the more apt I am to doubt my own judgment, and to pay more attention to the judgment of others."

Perfection, he said, was impossible. "When you assemble a number of men . . . you invariably assemble with those men all their prejudices, their passions, their errors of opinion, their local interests, and their selfish views. From such an assembly can a perfect production be expected? . . . Thus I consent, sir, to this constitution, because I expect no better, and because I am not sure that it is not the best."

Finally, he urged the delegates to keep to themselves the details of all the bickering that had taken place, to put aside any doubts, and to unanimously approve the document. But complete unanimity, Franklin knew, was not possible. Some delegates had said they would never sign. So Franklin proposed that the Constitution be approved by a unanimous vote of state delegations, which was done.

THE RISING SUN

As the delegates began to sign their names, Franklin looked at the chair on which Washington had sat as the convention's president. On the back of the chair was a painting of the sun. Franklin remarked to those near him that many times during the preceding months he had looked at the sun, as quoted by Van Doren, "without being able

Franklin's participation in the Constitutional Convention provided a much-needed sense of calm and collaboration. As with everything in his life, he approached this most important undertaking with intelligence, humor, and a willingness to compromise for the greater good.

to tell whether it was rising or setting. But now at length I have the happiness to know that it is a rising and not a setting sun."

By signing the Constitution, Franklin thus became the only person to have his name on the four most important documents in the creation of the United States: the Declaration of Independence, the treaty with France, the peace with Great Britain, and the Constitution. As with the first three, he had played a prominent role in the fourth. "The Constitution was not his document," writes Van Doren. "But without the weight of his prestige and the influence of his temper there might have been no document at all."

Once the Constitution had been signed, the story goes, a woman outside the statehouse stopped Franklin to ask him what kind of government the delegates had given the country. He answered, as quoted by Brands, "A republic, madam, if you can keep it."

The new Constitution would come under severe attack both from those who favored a stronger central government and those who wanted more state control. It finally became official when ratified by the ninth state, New Hampshire, in 1788. Washington became the nation's first president the following year. Franklin wrote Washington that having spent most of the last two years in pain was worth it, as quoted by Isaacson, "since they have brought me to see our present situation."

Franklin, indeed, was in almost constant pain from kidney stones, unable to travel and able to leave his house only with great difficulty. The only thing that brought relief was laudanum, which was a mixture of opium and alcohol. He was, however, philosophical about his condition. "People who live long," he said, as quoted by Isaacson, "who drink to the bottom of the cup, must expect to meet some of the dregs."

SLAVERY

His mind, however, remained sharp as ever, and even showed the ability to change. Slavery was one of the most divisive issues of the day. It was common throughout the colonies, not only in the South. As a young man, Franklin ran advertisements for slaves in his newspaper. When he became wealthier, he owned slaves himself.

He never really approved of slavery, but his early opposition was on economic, not moral grounds. He deplored the adverse effects on the masters. In 1751 he wrote, as quoted by Brands, "White children become proud, disgusted with labour, and being educated in idleness, are rendered unfit to get a living by industry."

By 1763 Franklin's view of blacks as inherently inferior to whites began to change. He visited a school for black children in Philadelphia and later wrote to a friend, as quoted by Brands, "I was on the whole much pleased, and from what I then saw, have conceived a higher opinion of the natural capacities of the black race, than I had ever before entertained. . . . I will not undertake to justify all my [prior] prejudices, nor to account for them."

Later, he was bothered that the ringing words of the Declaration of Independence about liberty did not apply to so many people in the new nation. Likewise, he only reluctantly accepted compromises on slavery in the Constitution. In 1787, prior to the passage of the Constitution, he accepted the presidency of the Pennsylvania Society for the Abolition of Slavery. In February 1790 the society presented a petition to Congress, perhaps written by Franklin, calling for complete abolition. It read, as quoted by Isaacson, that "the blessings of liberty" should be available "without distinction of color" and that Congress should free "those unhappy men who alone in this land of freedom are degraded into perpetual bondage."

The attack on slavery was Franklin's last act on the public stage. By March it was clear that he could not live much longer. His daughter, Sally, and her husband cared for him, as did his grandsons. The now-widowed Polly Stevenson and her children, whom he had convinced in 1786 to join him in Philadelphia, were also close by.

Some at his bedside tried to get him to declare his religious beliefs. He believed in God, he said, but that was about as far as he was able to go. As for the divinity of Jesus, he said, as quoted by Isaacson, that he was too busy to consider it now, but that "I soon expect an opportunity of knowing the truth with less trouble."

On April 17, an abscess in a lung burst and he was unable to speak. Later that night, surrounded by his two "families," Franklin died at the age of 84. Philadelphia gave its most celebrated citizen a huge sendoff; an estimated 20,000 people were in the funeral procession. The members of the U.S. House of Representatives wore black for a month in mourning. France paused in the midst of its own revolution to pay tribute to this most famous of Americans.

HISTORY'S VERDICT

History has not always been kind to Benjamin Franklin. His scientific accomplishments, it has been argued, were no more than those of a talented amateur. The real discoveries were made by others. His writings, notably the principled maxims put forth by Poor Richard, have been belittled by such figures as Herman Melville, Nathaniel Hawthorne, and Mark Twain. Writer D.H. Lawrence, quoted by Isaacson, referred to them as a "barbed wire moral enclosure." In politics, he has been condemned as being too quick to compromise, unwilling to take a heroic stand for his beliefs.

Such criticism, however, misses the point and the essence of Franklin's life and works. He was not interested so much in *great* as in *good*. His inventions were not intended to bring great benefits to humanity, but to make a better printing press, a more efficient stove, a brighter streetlight. Poor Richard was not intended to give sermons, only to share practical advice through which one could become a better, more productive person. If he compromised in politics, it was to accomplish the same thing as with his inventions—to make something useful. The Constitution is a perfect example; it was not what he wanted, but it might do the job, it was better than what had preceded it, and it was certainly better than nothing.

His diplomatic victories were as important in their way as those of George Washington on the battlefield. Franklin did not seek the total destruction of an enemy. Rather, he brought about situations in which both sides could exist.

What separated Franklin from most of the founders of the United States was that he did not take himself too seriously. Despite all his accomplishments he appeared to the world, and considered himself to be, a plain, straightforward tradesman. He could laugh at himself, and often did. Even in death, he made fun of himself. When he was 22 years old, he wrote what he hoped would be placed on his tombstone but never was. As quoted by Clark, it read,

The body of
B. Franklin, Printer
(Like the Cover of an Old Book
Its Contents torn Out
And Stript of its Lettering and Gilding)
Lies Here, Food for Worms.
But the Work shall not be Lost;
For it will (as he Believ'd) Appear once More
In a New and More Elegant Edition
Revised and Corrected
By the Author.

Chronology

1706	January 17 Benjamin Franklin born in Boston, Massachusetts.
1718	Franklin apprenticed to brother James, a printer.
1718	Franklin moves to Philadelphia.
1729	Franklin acquires *Pennsylvania Gazette*; son William is born.

TIMELINE

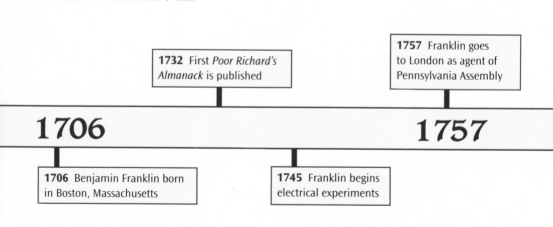

1732 First *Poor Richard's Almanack* is published

1757 Franklin goes to London as agent of Pennsylvania Assembly

1706

1757

1706 Benjamin Franklin born in Boston, Massachusetts

1745 Franklin begins electrical experiments

1730	Franklin and Deborah Read enter into common-law marriage.
1732	First *Poor Richard's Almanack* is published.
1743	Daughter Sarah (Sally) is born.
1745	Franklin begins electrical experiments.
1748	Franklin retires from active printing business.
1757	Franklin goes to London as agent of Pennsylvania Assembly.
1775	Franklin returns to Philadelphia and is elected to Second Continental Congress.
1776	Franklin helps edit Declaration of Independence and signs it on August 2.
1778	February 6 Franklin signs treaties with France.

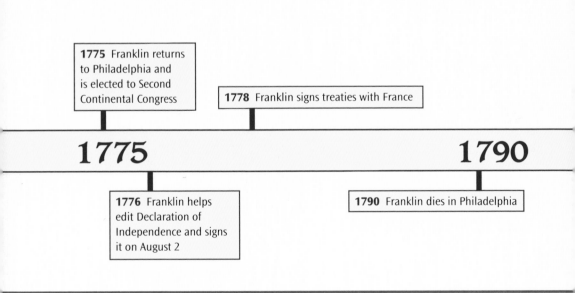

1775 Franklin returns to Philadelphia and is elected to Second Continental Congress

1778 Franklin signs treaties with France

1775

1790

1776 Franklin helps edit Declaration of Independence and signs it on August 2

1790 Franklin dies in Philadelphia

1782   November 30   Franklin signs peace treaty with Great Britain.

1787   Franklin achieves compromise on content of U.S. Constitution.

1790   April 17   Franklin dies in Philadelphia.

Bibliography

American Philosophical Society. "Franklin's Philadelphia," USHistory .org. Available online. URL: http://www.ushistory.org/franklin/ philadelphia/aps.htm.

Ashbrook Center for Public Affairs. "The Speech of Polly Baker," *TeachingAmericanHistory.org*. Available online. URL: http:// teachingamericanhistory.org/library/index.asp?document=469.

Avalon Project, Yale University Law School. "Preamble and Resolution of the Virginia Convention, May 15, 1776," Lillian Goldman Law Library. Available online. URL: http://avalon.law.yale .edu/18th_century/const02.asp.

Boese, Alex. "Trial of Polly Baker," MuseumofHoaxes.com. Available online. URL: http://www.museumofhoaxes.com/hoax/ Hoaxipedia/Trial_of_Polly_Baker/.

Brands, H.W. *The First American: The Life and Times of Benjamin Franklin*. New York: Anchor Books, 2000.

Clark, Ronald W. *Benjamin Franklin: A Biography*. Edison, NJ: Castle Books, 2004.

Franklin, Benjamin. "The Autobiography of Benjamin Franklin," Early America.com. Available online. URL: http://www.earlyamerica .com/lives/franklin/.

Isaacson, Walter. *Benjamin Franklin: An American Life*. New York: Simon and Schuster, 2003.

Lemay, J.A. Leo. *The Life of Benjamin Franklin*. 3 vols. Philadelphia: University of Pennsylvania Press, 2005–2008.

Morgan, Edmund S. *Benjamin Franklin*. New Haven, CT: Yale University Press, 2002.

Morgan, Edmund S. *The Birth of the Republic, 1763–89*. Chicago: University of Chicago Press, 1956.

Srodes, James. *Franklin: The Essential Founding Father*. Washington, D.C.: Regnery Publishing Company, 2002.

Van Doren, Carl. *Benjamin Franklin*. New York: Viking Press, 1938.

Wood, Gordon S. *The Americanization of Benjamin Franklin*. New York: Penguin Press, 2004.

Further Resources

BOOKS

Lloyd Yero, Judith. *The Declaration of Independence*. Washington, D.C.: National Geographic Society, 2004.

Marcovitz, Hal. *Benjamin Franklin: Scientist, Inventor, Printer, and Statesman*. New York: Chelsea House, 2006.

Meltzer, Milton. *The American Revolutionaries: A History in Their Own Words*. New York: Crowell, 1987.

Nardo, Don. *The Creation of the U.S. Constitution*. Detroit, MI: Greenhaven Press, 2005.

Owens, L.L. *Benjamin Franklin*. Edina, MN: ABDO Publishers, 2008.

WEB SITES

The Benjamin Franklin Tercentenary
http://www.benfranklin300.org
Interactive online version of an exhibit mounted in 2006 to celebrate the 300th anniversary of Franklin's birth.

The Electric Ben Franklin
http://www.ushistory.org/franklin
Comprehensive Web site dealing with all aspects of Franklin's life, work, and writing.

The Franklin Institute Science Museum. *Ben Franklin: Glimpses of the Man*
http://sln.fi.edu/franklin/rotten.html
Interesting interactive site for younger readers.

Picture Credits

PAGE

13: Mary Evans Picture Library / Alamy

18: Getty Images

24: *Benjamin Franklin, Printer, c. 1928* (oil on canvas), Dunsmore, John Ward (1856–1945) (after) /Collection of the New-York Historical Society, USA / The Bridgeman Art Library

30: Associated Press

41: Erich Lessing / Art Resource, NY

44: North Wind Pictures

48: Time & Life Pictures / Getty Images

54: Kevin O'Hara

61: North Wind Pictures

64: North Wind Pictures

78: Ivy Close Images / Landov

81: *Writing the Declaration of Independence in 1776* (oil on canvas), Ferris, Jean Leon Jerome (1863–1930) / Virginia Historical Society, Richmond, Virginia, USA / The Bridgeman Art Library

86: Library of Congress, Prints and Photographs Division, LC-DIG-pga-01591

92: Associated Press

97: Library of Congress, Prints and Photographs Division, LC-USZC4-9906

103: *Constitutional Convention* (watercolor on paper), Ferris, Jean Leon Jerome (1863-1930) / Private Collection / The Bridgeman Art Library International

Index

Page numbers in *italics* indicate photos or illustrations.

About the Author

WILLIAM W. LACE holds a bachelor's degree from Texas Christian University, a master's degree from East Texas State University, and a doctorate from the University of North Texas. He has written more than 40 nonfiction books for young readers on subjects ranging from the atomic bomb to the Dallas Cowboys. Lace lives in Arlington, Texas.